MODEL MARINE STEAM

MODEL MARINE STEAM

JOHN CUNDELL and JIM KING

ARGUS BOOKS

Argus Books Ltd
1 Golden Square
London W1R 3AB

© John Cundell & Jim King

© Argus Books Ltd 1983

First published 1983
Reprinted 1986

ISBN 0 85242 814 6

All rights reserved. No part of this book may be produced in any form or by any means without written permission of the Publisher

Typeset by M & G Studios Ltd., London NW10
Printed and bound in Great Britain by
The Garden City Press Ltd,
Letchworth, Herts SG6 1JS

Contents

	INTRODUCTION	7
1	STEAM FOR POWER	10
2	SIMPLE STEAM PLANTS	20
3	SLIDE VALVE ENGINES	30
4	PISTON AND OTHER VALVES	37
5	OTHER ENGINE DEVELOPMENTS	45
6	FIRETUBE BOILERS	53
7	WATERTUBE BOILERS	61
8	BOILER CONSTRUCTION	66
9	FIRING AND FUELS	76
10	AUXILIARIES	83
11	INSTALLATION AND MAINTENANCE	91
12	EXPERIMENTATION AND RADIO CONTROL	100
	APPENDICES	110

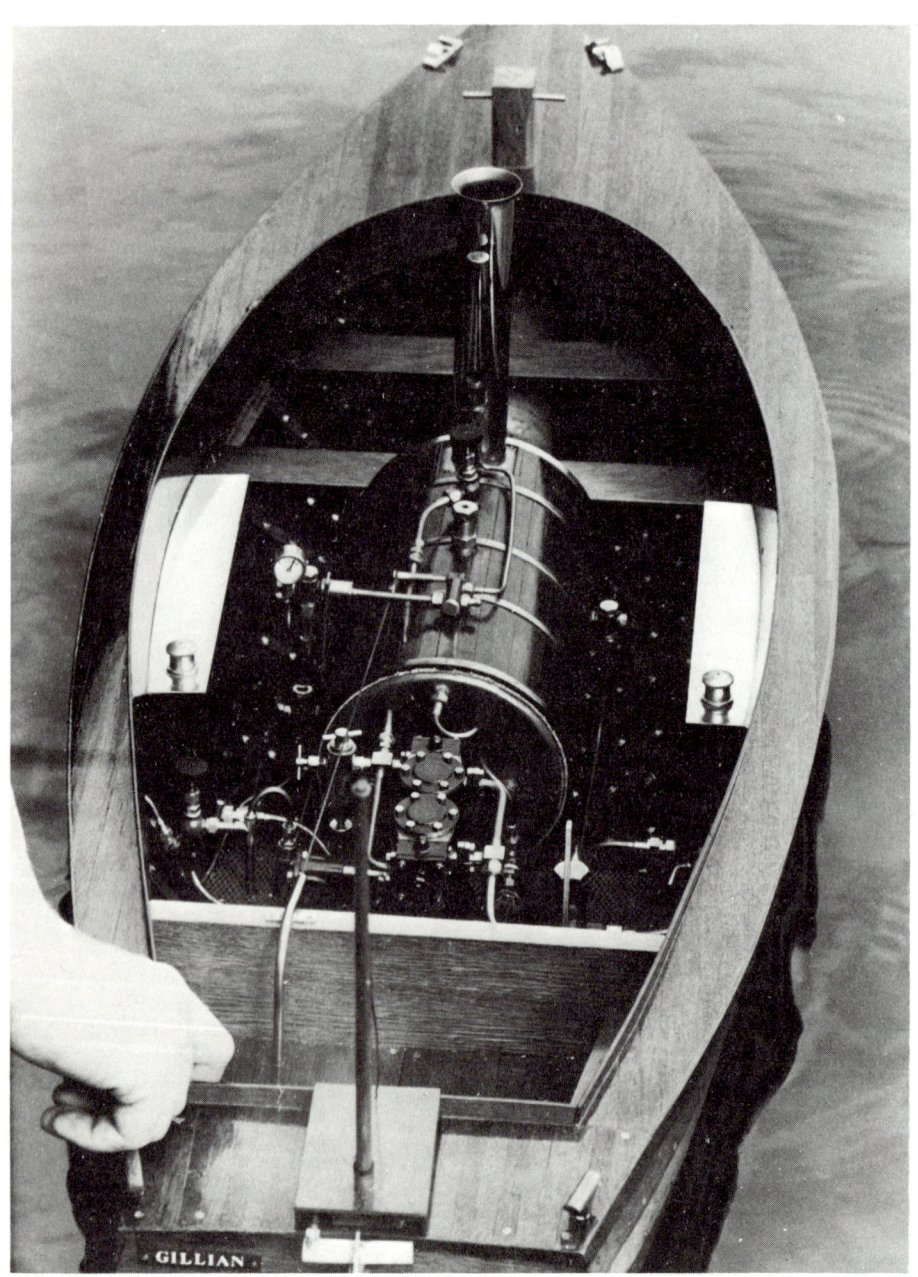

Introduction

Steam. The very word seemingly arouses the spirits of many people. Why is it? Nostalgia, perhaps, or because, alone of all the prime movers, steam power seems to be embodied with a form of life? Many hanker for the return of the steam locomotive with its highly emotive passage at speed, while others, not so old, can remember the engines in the many paddle steamers used for ferry and excursion purposes and, of course, many younger readers of this book will have already fallen under the spell of steam, if only by operating electrically driven steam-outline model locomotives.

Although the internal combustion engine has taken over many motive power requirements of transport, even today when large power units are required, steam is supreme, and most of the world's biggest ships and electricity generating stations depend on this source of power, albeit that the engine is in the form of a steam turbine. The turbine, like the internal combustion engine, does not have the same appeal as the reciprocating engine, and will only have a brief mention in these pages.

Steam as a source of power has served the human race for a long time; the ancient Greeks had some ideas (Hero's steam turbine is probable familiar to you, having been featured in the introduction to the subject of steam in most books) but as far as is known they never put their ideas to practical use.

Steam has always had a romantic appeal and the fable of James Watt watching the boiling steam in the kettle lifting the lid is well known, but like the story of Alfred and the cakes, it is probably some unknown writer's flight of fancy, for Watt, like so many pioneers, was a hard-headed business man and was probably not averse to supporting such ideas for his own ends.

Steam on the water was pioneered by such men as Bell on the River Clyde and Fulton in the United States of America, both initially making use of the inefficient stationary engines and boilers of the period adapted for marine use. From the middle 1800's full-size progress was rapid, and as always, there were men to model the full-size machine; in the world of model marine, events followed the prototype pattern.

Opposite, Gillian, a fine example of an open Victorian launch, fitted with a Stuart Turner Double Ten engine and a return tube boiler.

Introducing Model Marine Steam

Indeed, almost the first articles in the newly launched 'Model Engineer' of 1898 were concerned with marine steam. Particularly worthy of note in Volume 1 of that journal is a description of the building of a single-cylinder, double acting steam engine. The layout of the engine is one that is still common today.

In the early days of model power boating in this century there were two main sources of power, electricity and steam. For many years electric boats seemed to dominate the scene, probably because small motors and accumulators were readily obtainable. Just before the 1914-18 war, interest in model steamboats grew, and with many working in engineering factories and the advent of cheap lathes such as the famous Drummond Round Bed, the skills of daily work were put to good advantage by building boats and their engines. Between the wars, steam power became predominant, but then the commercial model internal combustion engine appeared on the scene and the first signs of a reversal of trends were apparent.

The early enthusiasts soon became famous for their exploits on the water with the aid of steam, and veterans still talk of the efforts by Ted Vanner of the Victoria Model Steamboat Club with his steam boat *All Alone*, Vines of West London, whose *Silver Jubilee* broke down into two halves for ease of transport, Bill Blamey with his steam outboard *Lil Men*; these are just a few of the well-known names in the London area. At the other end of the country, the North-East Coast clubs at Heaton and Tynemouth were a hotbed of enthusiasm for steam which has persisted until the present day. While most of the craft were designed for running on a straight course, aiming at a target and restricted in speed, there was a small band who followed the cult of the tethered hydroplane. Here the boat was raced on a circular course, tethered by a line to a central pivot. In this field, the boats powered by steam were star performers for many years, until the advantage gained by the better power/weight ratio of the internal combustion engine proved too much opposition. The steam hydroplane has not disappeared altogether from the scene though, and among present performers are veteran Arthur Cockman, whose series of *Ifit* boats dates from pre-1939, and post-war builder John Benson, co-author with Alan Rayman of the well-respected book, 'Experimental Flash Steam'. This small band of high speed engine builders struggles against long odds, but sometimes their achievements are spectacular, as anyone who witnessed the 70 m.p.h. runs of the late Bernard Pilliner's *Eega Beava* will testify.

So much for high speed, but the urge for speed was not felt by the majority of builders, and as expected, they followed the pattern of full-size craft in the engine rooms of their miniature marine fleets which in turn followed land-based practice. Beam engines were used for many years as side-lever engines in British ships, while many American ships had large beams towering above the decks, and these 'Walking Beam' engines, as they were known, lasted for many years, but gradually died out around the middle 1920s.

Beam engines for marine use were never very popular with the modeller, who generally modelled his engines after the patterns of the many steam launches that appeared on the scene. Some, more ambitious, copied the larger merchant navy engines, and both patterns have stayed with us.

Introduction

Semi-scale Strath trawler, 30 ins long by 5½ ins beam uses a small oscillator, solid alcohol fuel fired, which together with two channel radio control makes for an ideal introduction to steam power.

These types of engine, along with the humble oscillating engine, were sold by the model trade as castings, sets of machined parts or engines ready to run. From such firms as Whitney of City Road, The Model Dockyard, Aldgate, Bassett-Lowke of Northampton and Stuart Turner of Henley, the model mariner was well served. Only one of these firms still manufactures today, the makers of the world famous engines, Stuart Turner.

Engines of a simpler nature were produced in Germany by Märklin and Bing and there were some renowned oscillating engines by Bowman of Norwich. All have gone except Märklin, whose designs now appear under a different label.

Steam suffered a decline on our model oceans until recently, when the desire to get away from the noisy internal combustion engine revived the urge of marine modellers to make use of steam. In the following pages the well-tried patterns of the past will frequently appear, and it is hoped that the reader will find the text useful and helpful in the understanding of steam and its application to model marine. With diligence, it is possible for anyone to obtain satisfaction from a steam plant, but it is also appreciated that many modellers do not have the expertise or facilities to build all the parts of an engine-room.

As the object of this book is to encourage all to become expert master mechanics, many aspects of current supplies, i.e. basic castings, drawings, ready-to-assemble sets and completed plants will be touched upon, perhaps, because of the limits of space, not as much as the authors would like, but sufficiently to enable you successfully to start in this fascinating field.

Chapter One

Steam for Power

At the beginning of a book that is intended to increase awareness in steam, it seems reasonable to pose the question 'What is Steam?', because obviously an understanding of the power source that the modeller is to use will help in all his or her efforts. Most will say that steam is the vapour that is seen issuing from the spout of a boiling kettle, or leaking from the joints of a steam engine. This is true to a degree, except that in a pure state, steam is an invisible vapour, and the steam observed in the above examples contains minute drops of water to give it the visible cloudy appearance. Steam has the property of expanding considerably in volume when released from a higher pressure, and in so doing provides useful energy. This property will be impaired if water droplets are present, and in this condition steam is said to be saturated. To get the maximum power from steam it needs to be free of these water droplets, and to achieve this, extra heat (steam drying) is applied.

Like all heat engines, the steam engine will be more efficient the more heat the vapour contains, so modern practice is to add even more heat than that just required to dry it out and this is known as superheating. The limits to which we heat the steam and the pressure to which we raise it will depend on the purpose to which the engine is going to be put, the materials used and the efficiency of the lubrication system.

With a sufficient supply of steam, most engines will run irrespective of the condition they are in, and this is an advantage that the steam engine has over its nearest competitor, the internal combustion engine, which needs a better degree of construction and maintenance. This should not be an excuse, though, for allowing a steam engine to get into a bad condition, or even as an excuse for shoddy workmanship in the first place. Remember that good work always pays dividends with smoother, cleaner and more efficient operation.

In all dealings with steam, or to use a more impressive and perhaps more descriptive term favoured in the world of small locomotives, live steam, remember it is a medium that can be of some danger if mishandled and when operating any live plant, it is safety first and always.

In the sphere of model marine engineering the reciprocating engine is supreme; other types are so few in usage that they will only receive a brief mention in these pages. Before the reader attempts installation or construction of such an engine, it is essential to understand the workings and some of

Steam for Power

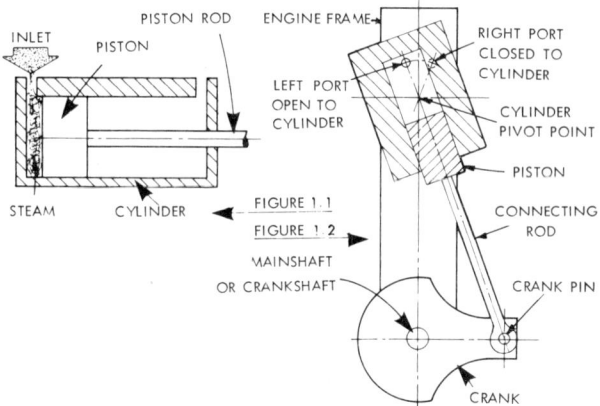

FIGURE 1.1
FIGURE 1.2

the terms associated with steam engines.

All engines of the reciprocating type have a piston moving to and fro in a cylinder (figure 1.1) under the expansive force of the steam. Steam has to be admitted and exhausted from the cylinder on each stroke of the engine, and some form of valve gear is needed to perform this function. In its simplest form this is done by having a port towards the end of the cylinder and oscillating the cylinder so that this port is alternately placed in line with another through which steam is admitted, known as the steam port, and also one which allows the steam to escape, the exhaust port. Figure 1.2 shows a typical layout of an oscillating engine, an explanation of which follows in Chapter 2. With such an engine using identical ports at equal positions in the cycle, reversing is a comparatively easy matter, for all that is required is a valve that will change over the steam and exhaust lines. This type of engine is one of the few that can make use of such a reversing valve, as most others need mechanical drive arrangements such as adjustable valve gears which are used for this purpose.

While the oscillating type of engine is relatively easy to construct, a short examination of the valve events will reveal that the expansion power of steam is not being used to best advantage. Steam is admitted some time after one of the dead centres (these are situated at the top and bottom positions of the crank when the centre lines of the piston rod and the crank coincide) and some of the steam always remains trapped in the cylinder. When oscillating engines were used for full-size use, the simple porting of our model engines was not practical, and a more sophisticated type of sliding valve mounted either on the side or end of the cylinder was used. Such a complication is not considered worthwhile by the majority of model marine constructors and indeed in the small size of engine being considered, it would be most difficult to make and operate such a valve gear satisfactorily. Model marine practice generally settles for the familiar fixed cylinder with slide or piston valve, and from observation, it is safe to say that the slide valve is the more popular choice by the amateur, the piston valve finding more favour with commercial engines of European origin.

The engines use for non-racing craft

Introducing Model Marine Steam

follow full-size practice very closely, though in a simplified form, being either close copies of the engines used in steam launches, with the cylinder block supported by turned columns, or similar to those used on the larger ships with cast columns. Both types follow a vertical format with the cylinder above the crankshaft. A large number of constructors use single cylinder oscillating engines, and for boats up to 30 ins. in length, a single cylinder double-acting engine of ⅝in bore by ¾in stroke would be satisfactory. For those not familiar with terms, the bore of a cylinder is the internal diameter, and of course is also the diameter of the piston. The stroke is the distance covered by the piston in going from one end of the cylinder to the other. A double-acting (D.A.) engine is one in which steam is applied alternately to both sides of the piston, while on the other hand, a singl- acting (S/A) engine is one in which steam is applied to the top of the piston only. While these terms may be familiar to many readers, in the course of a little research before commencing writing, it was found that there are a surprising number of people who are unaware of these matters, and if at some times the contents of these pages contain what would appear to be obvious items, please remember that all things are not obvious to all people.

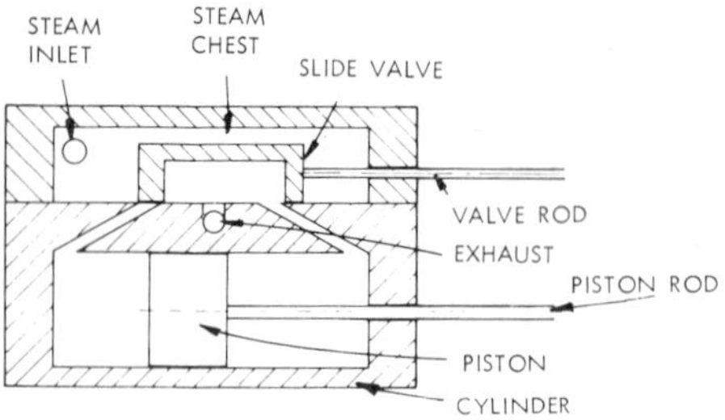

The more serious amateur constructors generally use a slide-valve engine and figure 1.3 shows a simple sectional representation of a slide valve cylinder. As can be seen, mounted on the side of the cylinder is a steam chest; the joint between the cylinder and the chest is machined flat and forms the valve face along which the slide valve, which has a cavity cast or machined into it, is driven to and fro by the valve gear. In the valve face are machined three slots, two being connected to either end of the cylinder by passages, while the middle slot is connected to the exhaust pipe. The compartment in which the valve moves is filled with steam from the inlet all the time the engine is in use. Piston valve engines are very similar in principle and when valve gears are discussed later on, more details of the operation will be give.

The commonest engines used are double-acting slide valve engines, single and twin cylinder, usually about ¾in bore and stroke, and driving boats up to about four feet in length depending on what sort of speed the owner wishes to achieve, and perhaps using a working pressure of 40lbs per square inch and upwards. There is a growing use of twin cylinder engines to power boats of 5ft or more in length, and when the cranks of the cylinders are set at 90°, one with the other, top and bottom dead centres of the individual cylinders are non-effective. This endows the engines with self-starting properties from any position of the crankshaft, making them most useful for radio-control where this facility is desired.

While the marine engine usually appears in the vertical form, there is plenty of scope for other arrangements, particularly when used for powering paddle steamers, and an inverted

FIGURE 1.3

12

Steam for Power

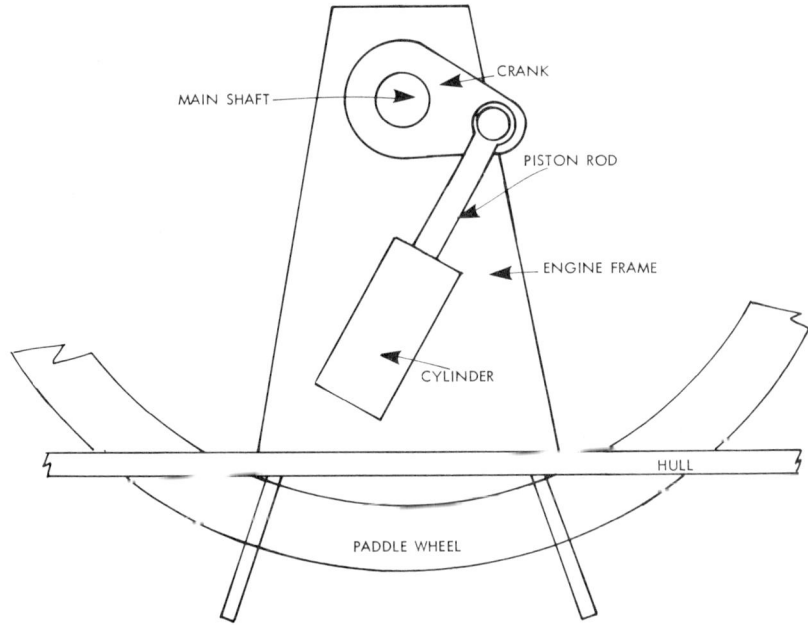

FIGURE 1.4 INVERTED OSCILLATING CYLINDER FOR PADDLE WHEEL BOAT

arrangement is shown in figure 1.4. More often than not an inclined design is more suitable, and one is shown diagrammatically in figure 1.5. It is an advantage in paddle steamers to have a long stroke engine and, in addition, the use of gearing to reduce the paddle speed is usually necessary, figure 1.6.

Horizontal engines can also be used with advantage when it is desired to get

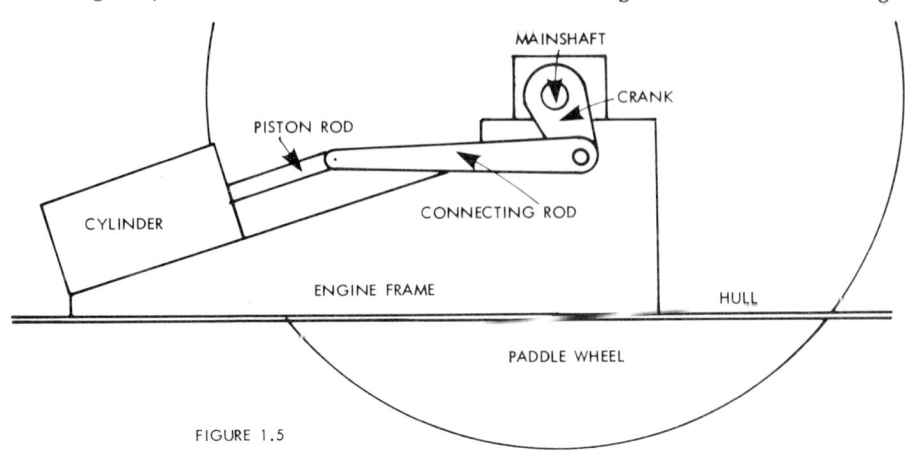

FIGURE 1.5

Introducing Model Marine Steam

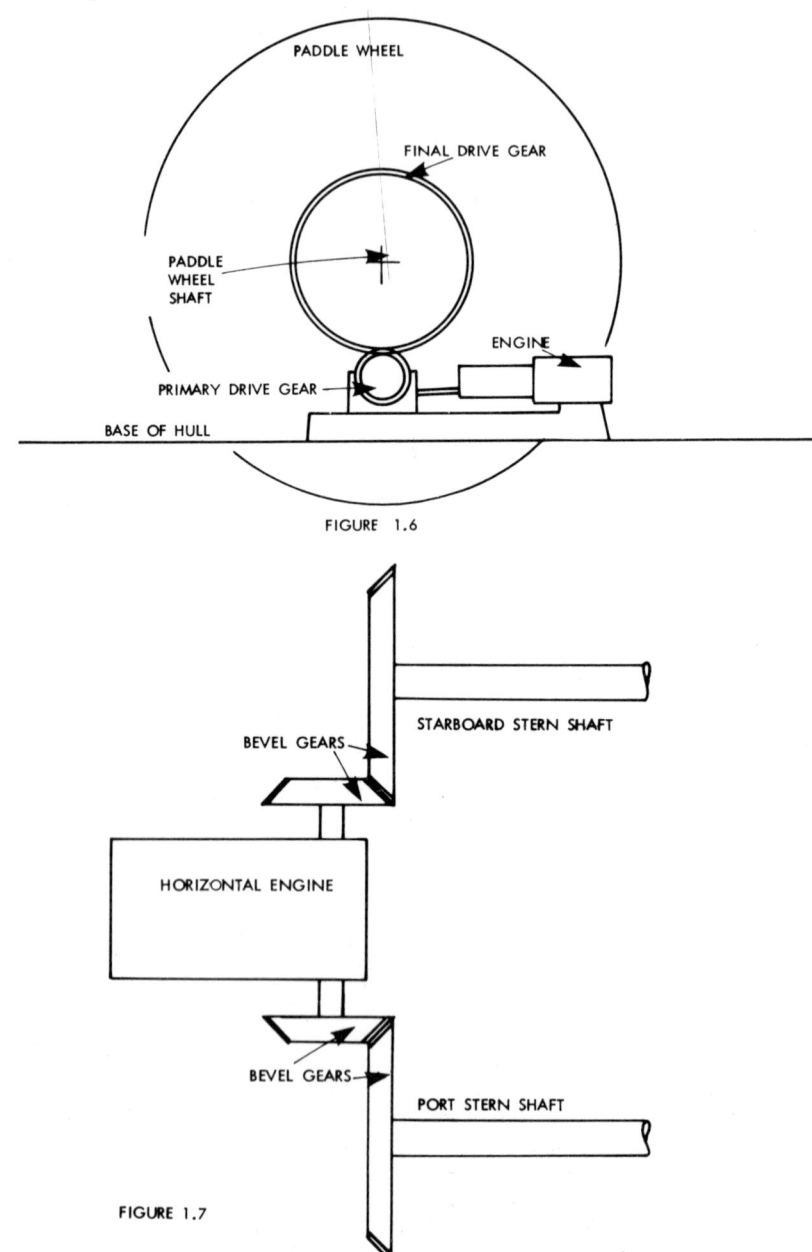

FIGURE 1.6

FIGURE 1.7

Steam for Power

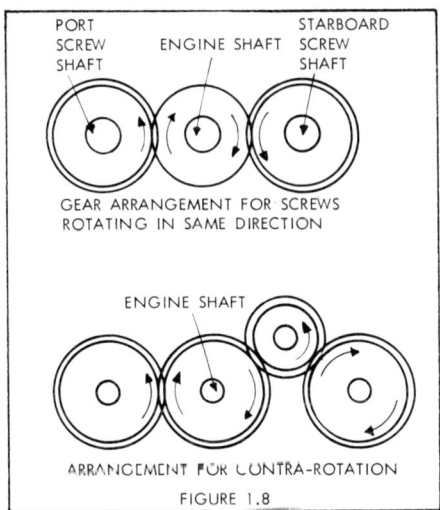

FIGURE 1.8

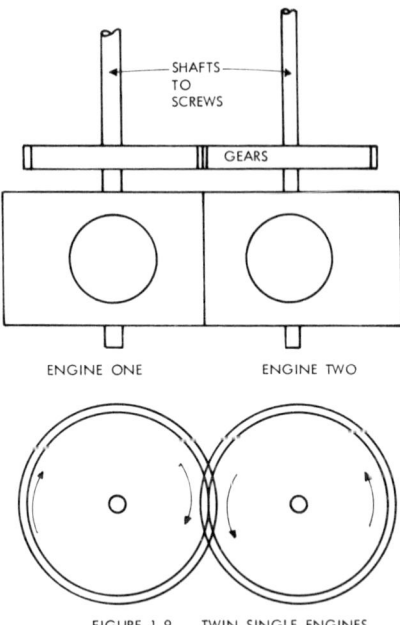

FIGURE 1.9   TWIN SINGLE ENGINES

weight as low as possible in a boat; by mounting bevel gears on either end of the shaft as shown in figure 1.7, twin screws can easily be driven. On the subject of twin screws, they are usually geared from a single engine, figure 1.8, but on larger boats, if two single cylinder engines are used side by side instead of a twin cylinder engine, figure 1.9, and geared together by equal sized gears, then both screws will rotate at the same speed in opposite directions. Of course, the individual valve arrangements of both engines must be set to suit. This arrangement saves lineal space in the hull; furthermore, if in a similar layout the engines are left uncoupled and separately equipped with throttles for each cylinder, then under radio control a highly manoeuvrable boat will be obtained.

It is worth while at this point to consider the use to which the engine is going to be put, and generally model steam boats can be assigned to one of three categories, i.e. scale models, functional models, or speed and racing boats. Of these three, most people start by building a boat that is strictly funct-

ional, in other words, the hull devoid of fittings unnecessary for the basic operation of the craft. The hull is essentially a container for the power plant, the whole being a simple arrangement which may or may not be built to resemble a full-sized craft. The next step usually leads to building a better scale ship or to go fully competitive and build another functional ship, perhaps more closely resembling a prototype, designed for running in straight course events.

Users of steam in scale models are often the subject of adverse criticism by the builders of so-called "true scale models", these being fully detailed and generally electrically propelled and including details that a steam model has to omit. You cannot have everything in this world, and the steam scale model has to sacrifice some finer detail to permit satisfactory operation, but then the builder has all the satisfaction that

15

Introducing Model Marine Steam

comes from a steam ship. Because they can be built to a large scale, tugs are great favourites for steam models, but this does not preclude other types, and next in the popularity stakes comes the steam yacht, which again can be built to a large scale. Merchantmen and liners are also to be seen on our inland oceans.

In all designs for steam boats, provision has to be made for a good flow of air to the burners, no matter what fuel is used, and this is one area where deviation from true scale has to be made. In some models, doors and skylights in the superstructure can be left open to assist ventilation. Another requirement is ready access to the boiler and machinery for normal running and in the case of emergency; therefore a large part of the superstructure has to be made as a removable unit(s).

Scale models in general do not need to be driven fast and the appearance of many a good ship on the water is spoilt by running it at too high a speed; to see an ocean liner or tug keeping pace with a destroyer to the same scale beggars comment. If just above scale speed is maintained, then the pressure in the boiler can be reduced with advantage. While there are many who work their engines at pressures of 80lbs/sq. in. and more, a larger number find pleasure and satisfaction with boiler pressures of half that.

In all marine construction, simplification pays off; the large complicated plant is all very well when it is working faultlessly, but the more complicated the plant is, the more things there are to be attended to, and also the more to go wrong. It should be a major objective to

The late Pauline Husband of the St. Albans Society with her twin screw, twin single-cylinder engined steamer, Lady of Mann.

Steam for Power

be able to handle the craft singlehanded once it is in the water. Most of the functional boats used in competition illustrate the point, for when competing, there is no time for attending to minor breakdowns, hence the designers tend to simplify layouts. Single or twin cylinder, single or double-acting engines are supplied with ample steam from slightly over-capacity boilers and in many cases even an engine driven boiler feed pump is omitted, feed water being supplied by hand pumping alone.

For those who would like to try their hand at straight course competitions, figure 1.10 shows the layout of a Model Power Boat Association straight-running course. Two type of competitions are held over this course. The Nomination Event requires the competitor to nominate the time his boat will take to cover the course. Placing is determined by percentage error of nominated time and actual time. The other competition is one of steering where boats are aimed at the target, and points scored according to which pair of buoys they pass through. Usually each competitor has three to five attempts, depending on the number of entries, at the target. Ties are resolved by re-runs. By the way, the scale model is not left out, for similar events are held for these types of steamships. For competitions on the straight course, the steamboat is particularly successful. One thing essential for success is to have the boats' engines running at as near as possible the same speed at each attempt in order that the turning effect due to the propeller and engine torque is always the same. This is not so easy with an I/C engined boat, but if the operating boiler pressure of the steam boat is arranged to be the same on each run, then it is logical to assume that the engine revolutions will be somewhere near the same on every outing.

The cult of the racing boat is very much a specialist one, and the practitioners in this side of model marine

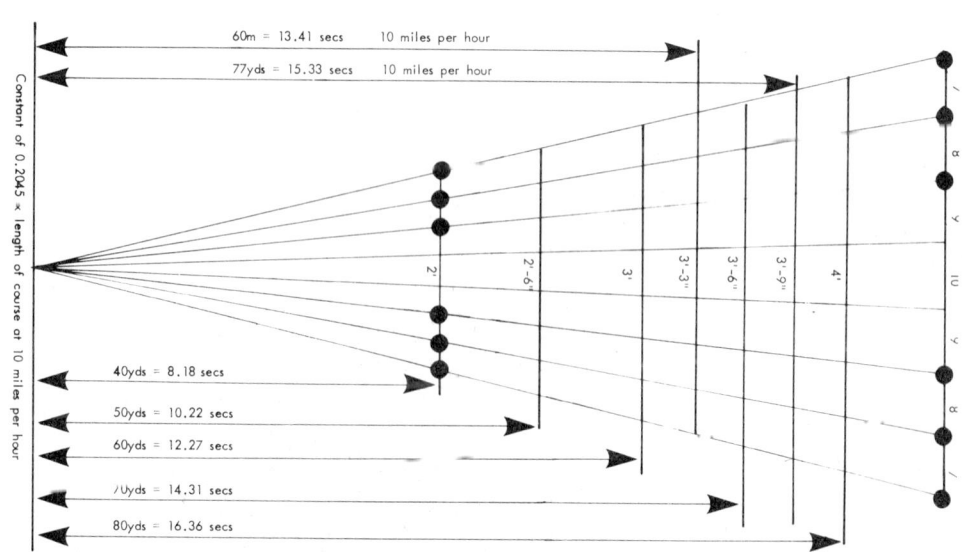

FIGURE 1.10

Introducing Model Marine Steam

sport have never been great in number but always very dedicated in purpose. Patience, resolution and excellent mechanical ability are needed at all stages in the design, building and operation of racing boats. This does not preclude a mention of current practice, for from the efforts of the seeker of high speeds and allied efficiency we can all learn a little. Generally, most boats used are of the three-point propeller-riding hydroplane type, figure 1.11, and most builders settle for a single cylinder single-acting engine with steam supplied from a flash steam boiler, although there have been a few boats built with steam turbines. Most builders find enough problems with the reciprocating engine without venturing into the realms of turbine technology, but it is on record that one turbine boat used steam that was so hot that the bearings had to be made of graphite and at pressures in excess of 3,000 lbs/sq. in. which turned the rotor at 250,000 revs per minute. It can be seen that the racing boat is very much a specialised part of the hobby, but if you feel so inclined, there is nothing to stop you following these dedicated modellers, for they started from the beginning like everyone else. Who knows, you may get pleasantly bitten by the hydroplane bug.

Whatever type of model marine engine you build, and whatever type of steamboat you instal the plant in, the earlier warning regarding safety is worth repeating. In building a steam plant, and in particular the boiler and blowlamps, make sure you follow approved practice and, until you have plenty of experience, build to a proved and published design. When you do decide to try out a design of your own, get it checked by someone with known experience.

Select your materials with care; if going to a well-known dealer with a

Fig.1·11 A three-point steam hydroplane for tethered running by Bob Kirtley of South Shields.

Steam for Power

Victoria Model Steamboat Club member Brian Munday prepares his steam powered straight running model, an example of a functional design.

reputation costs more than the odd-job shop or local scrapyard, then spend the extra money until such time as you are experienced enough to sort out the good from the bad.

In building boilers, always arrange to test or have them tested to a point where a good factor of safety is confirmed; twice times working pressure is recommended, but not so high as to strain the materials in use. Boiler fittings, safety valves, pressure gauges etc., should be tested at regular intervals during the running season, while boilers made of copper should be tested as described in detail in a later chapter.

Liquid fuels can always be a source of danger if carried in unsuitable containers; always use metal containers with screw caps, and never glass ones. The operation of pre-heating blowlamps can be fraught with danger at the lakeside if care is not taken during the process, and it is worth a warning to take added precautions if children are present.

Although it would appear obvious, some boaters ignore the fact that keeping a model power plant clean adds to the pleasure of running, and a regular clean-up operation mounted at the end of each run is well worth the effort. No apologies are offered if, throughout this book, the authors stress the importance of safety first and always, for with an increasing use of steam there is need for an increasing awareness of our responsibilities to other users of our lakes, and to the general public. It only needs someone to be careless and the whole hobby can suffer.

Chapter Two

Simple Steam Plants

The upsurge of interest in model marine steam is partly due to the importing of steam from West Germany and Japan. This activity by the model trade is not an entirely new development, for in the heyday of steam before the 1914-18 war and between the two World Wars, there were available to the modeller several reliable sources of supply of complete plants, ready-to-assemble kits and basic castings and plans. A look through the pages of past volumes of the 'Model Engineer' and even earlier publications will reveal that there has always been a strong commercial backing for the marine steam enthusiast.

In the days before they were bombed out during World War II, Whitney of City Road, London, made a series of single and twin engines, figure 2.1, of a design that found modern expression in Edgar Westbury's *Warrior* engine, drawings for which are still available. Bassett-Lowke made boilers and engines, and the boats in which to fit them, and some of the *Meteor* engines can still be seen in steamboats today. Another company alas no longer in business, Bowman of Norfolk, marketed a whole series of boats fitted with spirit fired boilers and oscillating engines. Their boats were very simple flat-bottomed launches and the whole concept was the sort of good toy that an uncle would buy for his favourite nephew. Nonetheless, the result was workmanlike and many a young mariner was set on his way with a Bowman launch. Figure 2.2 shows in outline the general shape of such a boat.

Possibly the most famous name in model marine steam, and one that is still with us, is Stuart Turner of Henley-on-Thames, whose pre-war range of complete plants, engines, sets of parts and castings were revived after 1945 and are among the best on the market today.

In former years, the products of Bing and Märklin and others came from Germany, but neither of the companies mentioned makes engines now; however, in place of the Märklin range we do have the Wilesco series, using what appear to be the same designs. One of their kits, suitable for the smaller boat, is shown in figure 2.3, while figure 2.4 shows the same plant installed in a model of the famous transatlantic paddle steamer *Sirius*. The layout shown is probably the simplest and most straightforward possible. The boiler and engine holding-down bolts are attached to the hull as shown in figure 2.4, and the components secured by nuts. This will allow easy removal of the engine or boiler for servicing. Care has to be taken in arranging the engine holding-down bolts in order that the centre lines of the crankshaft will

20

Simple Steam Plant

Fig. 2·1 *This oscillator, boiler etc. comprise the simplest of Stuart Turner range.*

Fig. 2·2 *A typical small steam launch of the Bowman type.*

Introducing Model Marine Steam

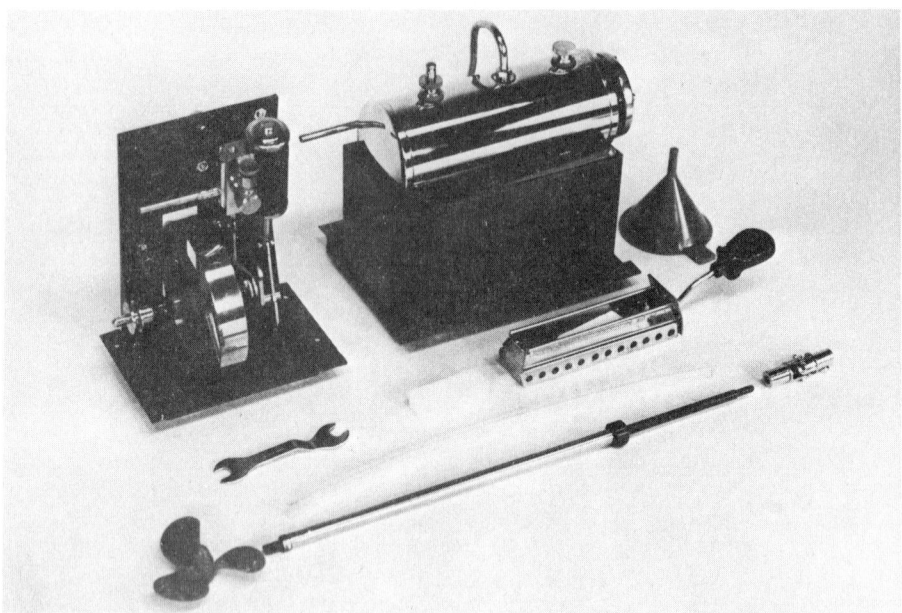

Fig. 2·3 A Wilesco commercial steamplant with, Fig 2·4 below, an installation in a paddle steamer model.

Simple Steam Plant

coincide with those of the propeller shaft, for although a universal joint is supplied with the kit, much power will be saved if accurate alignment can be achieved. With such a simple plant and hull combination many will find it easy to understand the needs of marine steam operation and gain experience for their next step.

G.H. Deason, in articles in 'Model Boats', described a suitable paddle boat and engine layout, the drawings for which are readily available, figure 2.5, and they will be found to be self-explanatory. While paddle boats are attractive vessels to model, the beginner should remember that there is more work in making the paddle wheels than in the

Fig. 2·5 A Mamod steam plant adapted to drive paddlewheels.

Alone among British manufacturers in this class of plant is one from the Mamod range of engines, which can be used in a similar way for your first steps. It is easily adapted for paddle use, as is also the Wilesco engine, and the unit is generally used for providing power for Meccano and similar construction sets, corresponding parts of a screw-driven ship, and also paddlers tend to be somewhat harder to manoeuvre than other types.

Japan entered the model marine steam engine market in the early 1970s and the Saito range became well known. Single, twin and three cylinder engines

23

Introducing Model Marine Steam

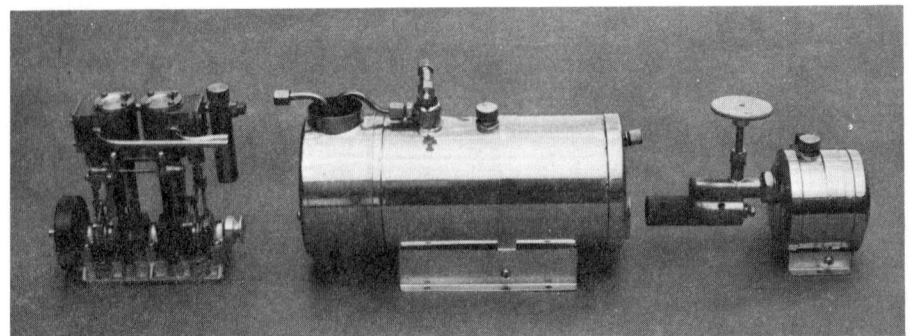

Fig. 2·6 A twin-cylinder engine and vaporising spirit burner in the Saito plant.

were available until 1981 with complementing boilers and spirit lamps and can still sometimes be found. All components were of brass construction and the range was among the most expensive on offer, which tended to detract from its attraction for the beginner. The engines and boilers could be installed in hulls in a similar manner to the Wilesco, and a Saito outfit is shown in figure 2.6.

Most of the requirements of the model marine engineer can be found in the Stuart Turner range, and most of their engines can be obtained in one of three different states of manufacture. Sets of parts, or individual items, are available as (a) un-machined castings and raw materials for the owner of a workshop with machining facilities, (b) as sets of parts requiring fitting and assembly, or (c) as complete ready-to-run engines. The simplest of their plants is the S.T., consisting of an oscillating engine of 7/16in bore x 7/16in stroke with a spirit

Fig. 2·7 This oscillator, boiler etc. comprise the simplest of Stuart Turner range.

Simple Steam Plant

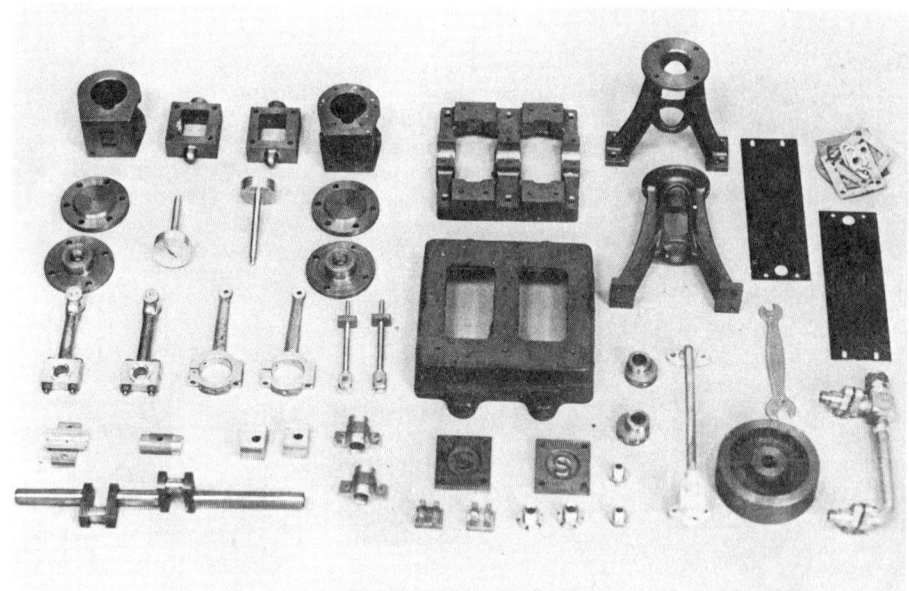

Fig. 2·8 Kit of machined parts for the Stuart Turner Double Ten.

fired boiler mounted on a wooden base, figure 2.7. Most will discard the base to fit the plant in the hull as described before. A better arrangement is to make a simple frame of aluminium or brass angle to accept the units and arrange to fix this to the hull with three or four bolts or U clamps and brackets, so that the whole can be removed as one.

Somewhat more complicated and better known than the S.T. engine is the Stuart No. 10; this well tried product of the Henley-on-Thames works is a ¾in bore x ¾in stroke D/A slide valve vertical engine, and is to be seen in boats all over the world. It has proved most satisfactory as a prime mover for boats up to four feet overall, and the cylinder castings on their own have been the basic elements in many a home-designed engine. A development of the S.T.10 is the Double 10, and this has been selected as a good example of model marine practice. Figure 2.8 shows the kit of machined parts as supplied and it should be noted that the S.T. 10 is similar except for a smaller baseplate and a smaller number of components. Figures 2.9 to 2.12 show stages in the assembly. The completed engine will power some ships of 60in or more in length, depending on the hull form and the speed at which it is desired to run the ship. Until recently, neither the 10 nor the Double 10 were available with reversing gear, which somewhat restricted their use for radio-control, but this omission has now been rectified and unmachined parts are available.

Machined sets of parts from Stuart Turner's require some hand finishing and fitting, nothing to be scared of, and this provides a good general exercise for those who would like to improve their skills, and provided that like all good fitters they remember that patience is a virtue, and follow that precept, then indeed virtue will be rewarded. Many

Introducing Model Marine Steam

Figs. 2·9 – 2·12

other good engines come from Henley-on-Thames, and a look through Stuart's catalogue is time well spent.

For those with the requisite workshop facilities, Reeves of Birmingham have some good sets of castings including several for designs by Edgar Westbury, whose name is well known to many of the older generation as a most competent designer. A set of castings for a *Warrior* engine to his design is shown in figure 2.13. Also among the sets offered by Reeves is one for an oscillating engine, and figure 2.14 shows the general arrangement and figure 2.15 gives an idea of the number of parts needed

The oscillating engine will be for many a first project, and whether the engine is bought ready to run, as a set of castings, or built from strip and tube material, an explanation of its operation will not come amiss. This type of engine makes use of cylinder movement to open and close steam and exhaust ports, and is shown in diagrammatic form in figure 2.16. In these engines the piston is fixed rigidly to a connecting rod driving on to a crank and so turning a crankshaft. As the shaft turns and the piston moves in the cylinder, the cylinder will oscillate on its fixed pivot point. The cylinder has a flat face in which is drilled a single hole (port), and this face matches and oscillates over a fixed valve face which has two holes drilled in it which, at the extremities of the cylinder's swing, will line up with the cylinder port. Steam is admitted through one, the steam port, and escapes through the other, the exhaust port. It is easy to see that depending on which port is used for either purpose, the engine will rotate one way or the other. If a change-over-valve is fitted in the steam and exhaust lines, the engine can be operated in either direction at will. As shown, the engine is single-acting (S/A) but if the

Simple Steam Plant

Fig.2·13 A set of castings for the Warrior engine from Reeves at Birmingham.

piston is arranged so that steam can be admitted below the piston, it would be double-acting (D/A). To achieve this, another pair of ports are arranged below the first mentioned set, to line up with another port in the cylinder.

Oscillating engines are often derided as a form of power, and indeed in many cases there is justification for adverse criticism, but by exercising care in construction and maintenance, many of the causes of trouble and poor efficiency can be eradicated.

The port layout, simple though it is, is often a prime cause of trouble and for those who wish to make an engine from materials at hand, the following simple explanation of the port arrangements

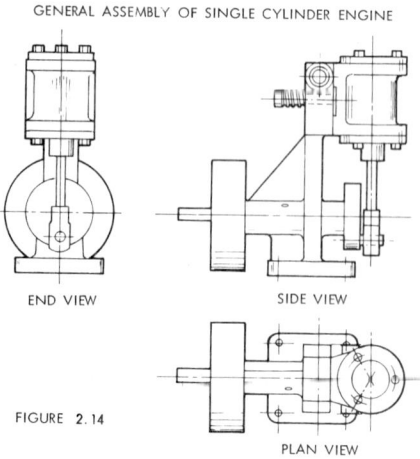

FIGURE 2.14

Left, Fig. 2·14, a simple oscillating engine
Below, Fig 2.15, castings for the engine.

27

Introducing Model Marine Steam

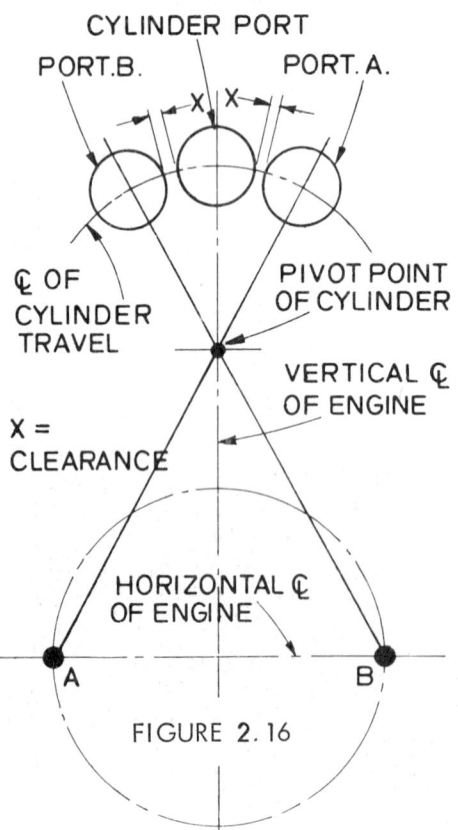

FIGURE 2.16

Above, perhaps the simplest form of steam power; the 'pop-pop' engine. Heating the copper coil with a solid fuel tablet causes alternating pressure and vacuum pulses which will propel a small model.

will be of use; even those who will buy an engine or perhaps build one from someone else's plans might find it of interest.

To set about laying out the ports, draw to as large a scale as possible an enlargement of the engine pivot points as in figure 2.16; on the horizontal centre line of the engine, mark the two extreme points of the crank through "A" and "B". Mark the pivot point of the cylinder on the vertical centre line and draw two lines from points "A" and "B" through this point. Depending on the stroke and the length of the piston, one can then determine the centre line of the cylinder port travel. The diameters of the ports will then be one half of the distance between the centre points of the column ports, less a distance "x" required to prevent an overlap of the three ports at the top and bottom dead centres. Many designers arrange that no clearance is allowed. Providing that ports are drilled accurately to size, this works satisfactorily, but when some inaccuracy creeps in, some clearance is an advantage.

Simple Steam Plant

One of the most usual causes of steam leakage happens when the cylinder pivot and the crankshaft are out of parallel, for it will be seen that this offset will cause the cylinder face to move away from the column face, so releasing steam from the inlet pipe. A good sliding match of the two valve faces is an essential for success and even if the engine is a commercially produced one, it pays to keep an eye on this and if necessary remate the surfaces occasionally. Keep the faces clean and make sure that engine lubrication is good. On this last point, it is worth noting that one of the best of pre-war suppliers of engines, Bowman, used a drip-feed oiler that was positioned above the valve faces, but more later of lubrication, which is vital to all engines.

To hold the two faces together, a spring-loaded pivot pin is used and care is needed to ensure that the pressure imposed is sufficient to hold the faces together against the steam pressure, but not so heavy that undue pressure is imposed, causing friction and loss of power. While as said before, we are not too worried about the engine's efficiency, these small points collectively will improve performance and reduce the loss of steam within the hull.

A modern version of the ever-popular oscillating engine is the U.S.E. engine, which can be used singly or combined to create multiple engines like this V8.

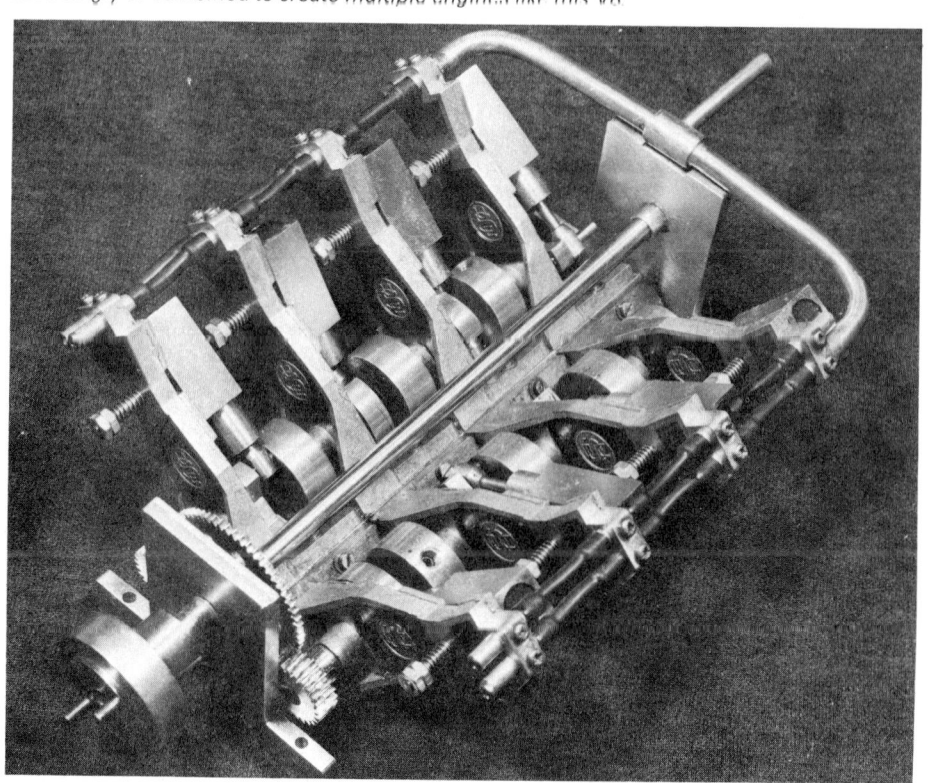

Chapter Three

Slide Valve Engines

It does not take long to appreciate that the oscillating engine has several disadvantages that become more noticeable as the engine is used. Among these are a propensity to steam wastage due to not using its expansive power to the fullest extent, and also steam leakage which becomes worse as wear develops, and if used in a radio-controlled boat can pose problems from humidity and heat. Full-size practice long ago abandoned the un-enclosed sliding valve of simple model engines and then later the oscillating cylinder, in favour of a fixed cylinder with an enclosed sliding valve driven from the crankshaft. The ensuing layout made for better use of the steam and gave increased power and economy.

To gain an idea of how a slide valve engine works, first look at figure 3.1 which shows in simple form a section of the cylinder arrangement. Attached to the side of the cylinder is a steam chest which is kept filled with steam all the time the engine is working, and in which the slide valve operates. Machined on the side of the cylinder is a flat valve face, along which the slide valve moves and in this face are machined three slots, figure 3.2. The middle one is connected to the exhaust pipe and forms the exhaust port, whilst the other two ports are connected by passage ways to either end of the cylinder. As the valve is moved along its face, the cylinder ports are alternately opened to steam and exhaust. Live steam is admitted directly from the steam chest as the exhausted steam at the other end of the cylinder is directed via the cavity in the valve to the exhaust port. The valve is normally held to its face by the live steam pressure, although some builders also load the valve with a flat spring.

In the form shown, and also in figure 3.3, it will be seen that the cylinder is open either to steam or exhaust, and therefore the steam will not expand as is desired for efficient operation. In order to obtain the needed expansion of the steam, it is necessary to add an overlap to the valve, figure 3.4, and by so doing the admission of steam is cut off when the piston is on its way down the cylinder. From the point of cut-off until the end of the stroke, the cylinder is closed to both steam and exhaust, and all the power in driving the piston comes from the inherent expansive force of the trapped steam.

The amount by which the valve overlaps the outside edges of the cylinder port in mid-stroke is defined as the lap of the valve, and the point at which steam is cut off is usually given as a percentage of the total amount of steam that would

Slide Valve Engines

be consumed if no cut-off were made until the end of the stroke, i.e. if the valve closed with the piston having covered one quarter of the stroke, then the cut-off would be 25%.

In order to get most effect, steam is usually admitted to the cylinder port slightly before the piston reaches the end of the stroke, a factor known as lead, and because of this, some compression occurs in each stroke. The cycle of events occurring in the cylinder is therefore steam admission – steam cut off – steam expansion – exhaust (in which some compression will occur) – compression. Lead is not generally considered of much consequence in slow running engines, but when high speeds are

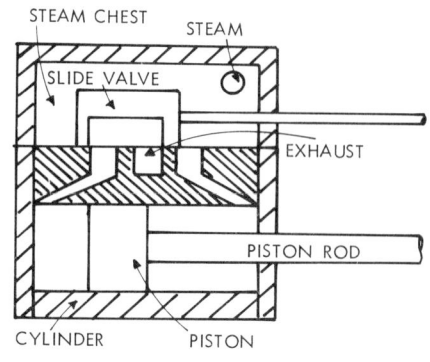

FIGURE 3.1

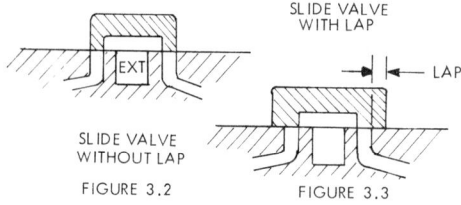

FIGURE 3.2   FIGURE 3.3

attempted it becomes a useful factor to incorporate. In order to clear steam quickly some engines include exhaust clearance. This is an amount by which the valve would be open to exhaust in its mid-position, however this is a design item which we can ignore, for in slow running engines it would be a most wasteful addition for it allows the possibility of inlet steam to pass direct to exhaust.

All these factors need to be taken into account if the reader decides to go more deeply into engine design, but it is assumed that for the time being existing designs will be selected.

So far so good; we now have a reasonably effective method of controlling the steam into and out of the cylinder, and next we need a means of guaranteeing synchronisation with the piston. The method most used is by an eccentric fixed on the crankshaft, driving via an eccentric rod, the valve rod, figure 3.4. The eccentric is a disc mounted on the crankshaft and as the name implies, is out of centre. The distance between the centre of the eccentric and the centre of

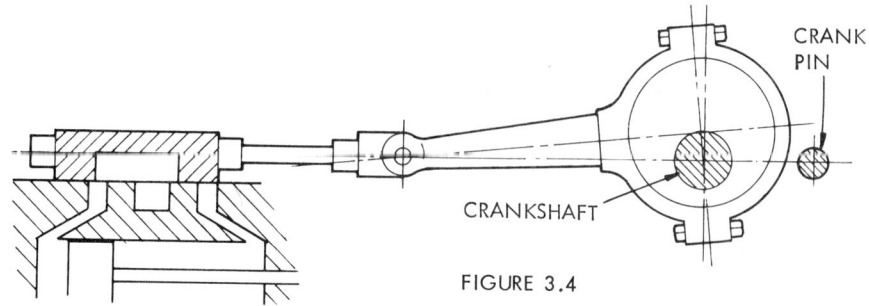

FIGURE 3.4

31

Introducing Model Marine Steam

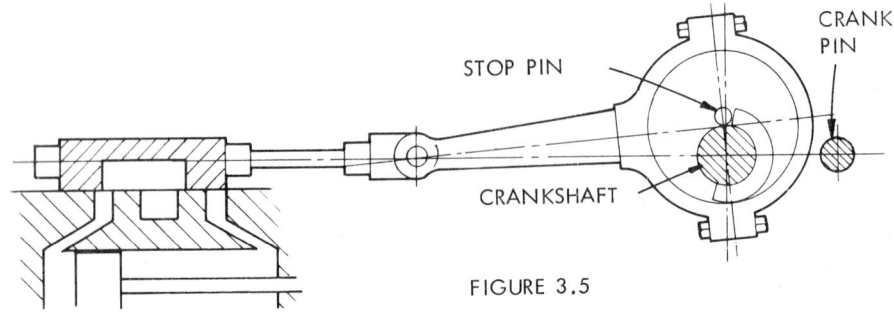

FIGURE 3.5

the crankshaft will equal one half the total travel of the slide valve and it is easy to see that as the engine turns, this out-of-centre movement will cause the slide valve to move backward and forward. The eccentric is set in advance of the crankpin. For a valve without lap this angle of advance would be 90°, but this is increased for a valve with lap in order to have steam admitted at the right point in the cycle of events. While the eccentric is the most commonly used means of driving the valve, it is possible to make use of a secondary crank fixed to the crankpin to give the required drive. This method is not often used in model marine engines but for those interested,

the arrangement can be seen in pictures of outside cylinder/valve gear locomotives.

Of course, with this simple arrangement no reversing of the engine is possible, but since boats that are used for free running without radio control are not usually sent astern, this is no disadvantage and 90% of such boats make use of the simple eccentric drive.

In order to enable the engine to run in either direction with this simple eccentric drive, a modification is required and the arrangement used is shown in figure 3.5, and is known as a slip eccentric valve gear. In this arrangement, the eccentric is made a loose fit on the crank-

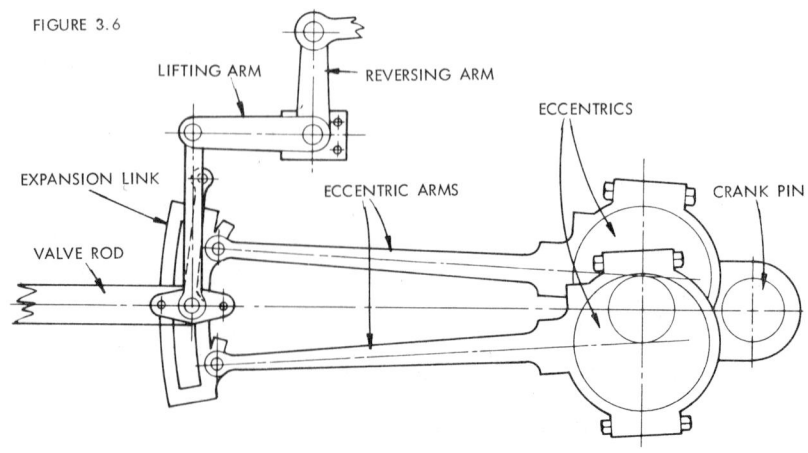

FIGURE 3.6

Slide Valve Engines

shaft and a collar suitably cut away as shown is mounted beside the eccentric and drives a pin fitted to the eccentric. To reverse the engine, steam is shut off and the crankshaft turned by hand in the required direction of operation. Lap and lead can be given to the valve as with the simple eccentric. The arrangement suffers from the need manually to reverse the crankshaft. The gear is not often used in model marine practice for this reason, but commercial engines such as the Wilesco, figure 2.3, intended for a variety of uses, often have a slip eccentric.

While the majority of slide valve engines used in model ships have the valves driven by the single eccentric, many builders like to have reversing gear fitted to their engine, even though in many cases and particularly with craft not under radio control, the facility is never used. The solution to the problem of reversing a steam engine plus the need in commercial use to be able to vary the cut-off point of steam admission taxed many minds, and the result was a great variety of design for valve gears. Isaiah Howe, who was employed as a foreman by Robert Stephenson, invented a gear for controlling the slide valve many years ago in the early days of steam locomotion, and like many such designs, they still exist today. This gear, now known as "Stephensons Valve Gear", is almost universally used on the reciprocating marine engine, although its application on locomotives, for which it was designed, is generally restricted to use between the frames.

Figure 3.6 shows diagrammatically the general layout of Stephensons Valve Gear. There are two eccentrics, one set for ahead running and the other for astern. They are pivoted to either end of a curved expansion link. This link is coupled and pivoted to a lifting link which can be moved by the reversing lever. Movement of the lifting link causes the expansion link to move from one position to the other in order to bring the required eccentric in line with the valve rod. The valve rod has a die shaped to fit the slot in the expansion link and is moved by the action of the relevant eccentric. It is set in place by the position of the expansion link, and thus it can be seen that the amount of movement of the valve will vary according to the position of the die in the expansion link, so varying the amount of cut off.

While Stephensons Valve Gear is the one that marine engineers generally use, there are other gears that may prove attractive in some circumstances. Gears that operate without, or only partly with the use of the eccentrics, are radial valve gears, and also among those that have found favour in the past is the Joy Valve Gear. As can be seen from figure 3.7, the valve is driven from a combination of links deriving their motion from a pivot point on the connecting rod. This gear could be used with satisfaction in a stern wheeler, where the paddle wheel is driven directly by a crank mounted on the paddle wheel shaft.

Referring again to figure 3.7, which shows the gear in midposition, in order to put the gear in forward or reverse, the reversing arm is moved to the left or right, and it will then be seen that as the crank turns and the centre of the connecting rod (known as Pitman in the U.S.A.) moves up and down, so will the die in the slide, and this in turn moves the valve spindle back and forth. The timing of the valve is set by the layout and proportions of the several links of the gear.

Joy's Valve Gear suffers a slight design disadvantage in normal use because of the need to take the initial drive from the connecting rod, and unless this rod is enlarged at the connecting rod

Introducing Model Marine Steam

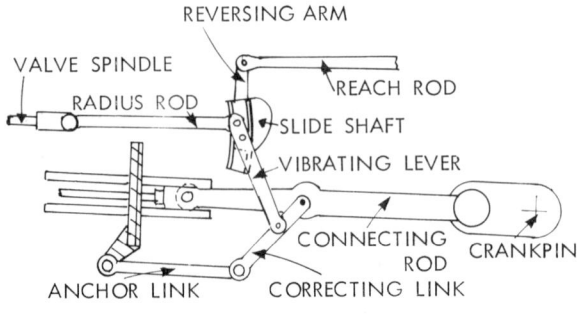

FIGURE 3.7

pivot, then fractures can occur. In the case of a model stern wheeler, no problem should occur, for the prototypes usually had this component fabricated from one or more baulks of timber, and reproduction in an aluminium alloy should give sufficient strength.

Since this book is intended as a primer for the budding model marine engineer, the layout design of sophisticated valve

This 8ft long model of S.S. Great Britain features a Stuart Turner Double Ten engine, centre flue boiler and gas burner by Treetower and two channel radio control. (Photo by Ray Brigden).

Slide Valve Engines

Stuart Turner's triple expansion engine, this one built by Bert Perman.

gears will not be covered in these pages, but for those who wish to try their hand at design, then reading of those books devoted to small locomotive practice will be most rewarding and points of design will be found covered in more detail than can be afforded in these pages.

Both Stephenson's and Joy's Valve Gears make use of curved links which sometimes cause headaches in construction. There are various ways of making links for the open one, figure 3.8. Probably the simplest method most likely to be used is as follows. Mark out the link, including the curved centre line of the slot. Then centre punch along the centre line and drill a series of holes, figure 3.9, break out the unwanted metal and finish with files to the marked lines.

It may sound a difficult process but many hundreds, nay thousands, of links have been made in this way. The use of a watchmaker's eyeglass will be of help in the final stages, and for smooth operation, the surfaces along which the die

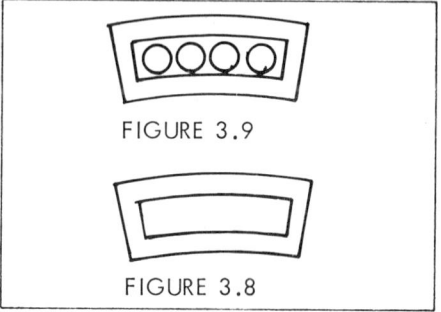

FIGURE 3.9

FIGURE 3.8

35

Introducing Model Marine Steam

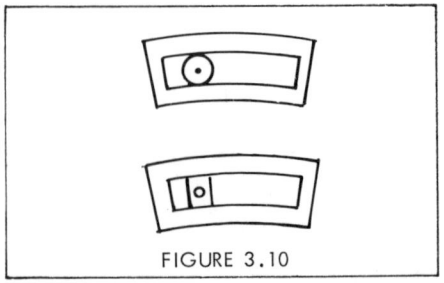

FIGURE 3.10

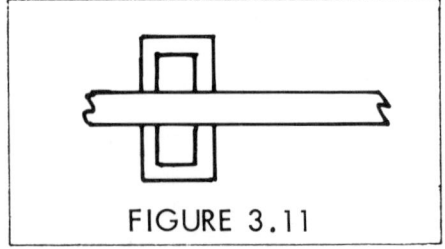

FIGURE 3.11

travels must be as good as you can make them. The die block should receive the same careful attention, and one should not be tempted to substitute a simple circular pin or even a ball-bearing for the awkward shaped die block as this item requires as much of its surface bearing on the expansion links as possible, figure 3.10.

Of course, those with the requisite equipment can set up the link on a vertical miller and end-mill the slot, while if double or single slotted links are used with the die block working in the slot, (figure 3.11 shows a plan view), then a ring of metal can be set up on the faceplate of the lathe and the curved slot turned. As many links as required can then be cut off.

The curved expansion links of both gears and the two eccentrics of Stephenson's tend to deter some people, who may therefore be attracted to a valve gear that has only one eccentric and a straight guide.

There is such a gear, the Hackworth, figure 3.12, which has often been used in both large and small locomotive work, but for some reason it does not often appear in marine engines. As seen in the figure, there is an eccentric which moves a die to and fro along a slotted link, which is itself pivoted in the middle. Connected to the eccentric rod is the radius rod which drives the valve. Which way the link slopes will determine how the valve will be moved in relation to the piston, and this therefore determines which way the engine will turn.

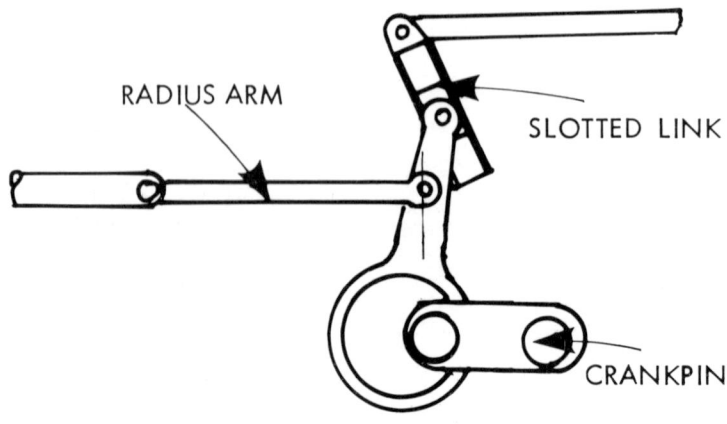

FIGURE 3.12

36

Chapter Four

Piston and Other Valves

For most purposes the slide valve will satisfy all requirements as it is simple to make, its action is easily understood, if well lubricated it is long wearing and reliable, and when re-conditioning is necessary then machining of the faces is easy. For all these reasons it remains a popular choice for most model marine engineers. In full size practice, as engines increased in size and required speeds rose, the slide valve became less popular because of the power absorbed by its inherent weight and increased valve face contact pressures, caused by higher steam pressures.

Improved forms of slide valves were devised, e.g. in the balanced valve type the valve was held to the face by spring pressure without the steam bearing down on the slide valve, but by and large engineers sought new valve forms for major improvements.

One of these replacements, most used in locomotive work and to some extent in commercial model marine, is the piston valve, of which there are generally two types. These are inside and outside admission, but we need only concern ourselves with the inside admission type for amateur construction.

Figure 4.1 shows a section of the cylinder with an outside admission piston valve, and it can be seem that effectively it is a cylindrical slide valve. Steam is admitted through the entries at either end of the valve chamber and is diverted to either end of the cylinder by the bobbin, as the latter is shuttled to and fro by the valve gear. Used steam is exhausted through the turned-down centre of the bobbin in a similar manner to the slide valve, and exhausts to atmosphere via the orifice at centre of chamber.

LAP AND LEAD

Lap and lead can be given to a piston valve in the same way as with a slide valve. Lead is obtained in exactly the same manner, and lap is given by a similar thickening of the end portions of the bobbin, as is done with the end walls of a slide valve. Figure 4.2 shows a typical example.

While to the prototype designer the piston valve has many attractions, for many amateur engineers, unless they are gifted with expert machining ability, the humble slide valve is to be recommended. Piston valves require in the first instance good fitting to maintain a steam-tight operation. It is almost essential for efficient operation that rings are fitted to take up wear, and even more essential in the case of this valve is the need for good constant lubrication. The foregoing is not meant to deter any-

Introducing Model Marine Steam

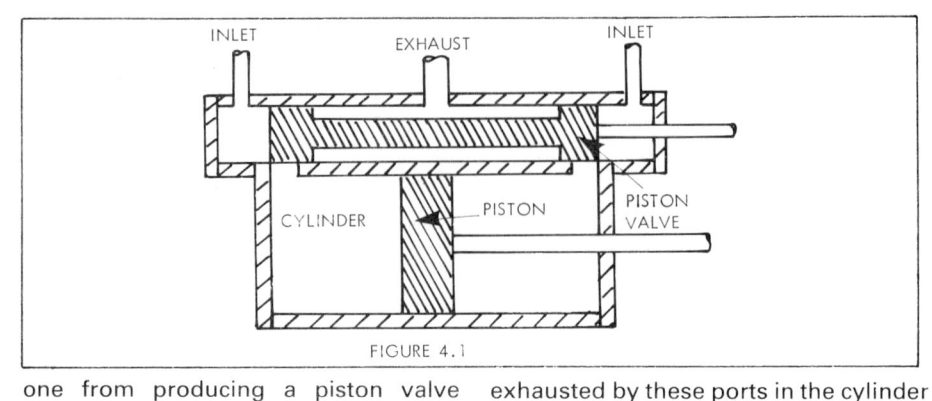

FIGURE 4.1

one from producing a piston valve engine, but for those who do attempt the job, remember that good workmanship is essential; the valve chamber needs to be bored, as any suggestion of a simple drilling job is ruled out from the start. The bobbin needs to be a good fit, again with rings being fitted to take up wear. The drive spindle has need of clearance in the bobbin but the driving collars have to have minimum play.

So far it has been assumed that the valve is to be fitted to a double acting cylinder, but often the piston valve is used for single acting work, quite often in conjunction with auxiliary ports for high speed use. Figure 4.3 shows such an arrangement. The steam inlet and the main exhaust are controlled by the piston valve. As soon as the main piston reaches the bottom of its stroke, steam is exhausted via an auxiliary set of ports in the cylinder walls. In some designs of engines the whole of the steam is exhausted by these ports in the cylinder walls, and since in this case the steam flows in one direction only, the system is known as a "Uniflow" one.

While both piston and slide valve engines are usually designed so that the valve chamber is parallel to the cylinder, sometimes the valve chamber is part of the cylinder head. Figure 4.4 shows an arrangement using a piston valve for twin single-acting cylinders. The arrangement is not practical for double-acting cylinders. Drive can be from an eccentric mounted on the crankshaft through a bell crank or by gears driving a horizontal eccentric in line with the valve centre line. Stuart Turner's *Sun* and *Sirius* engines make use of such an

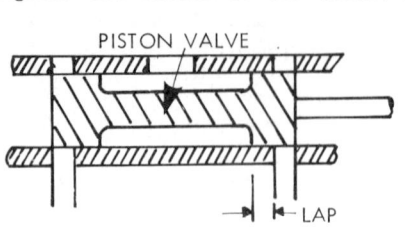

FIGURE 4.2

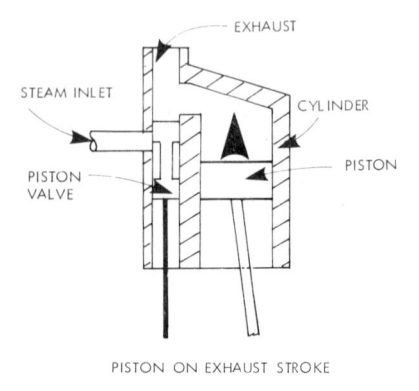

FIGURE 4.3

Piston and other Valves

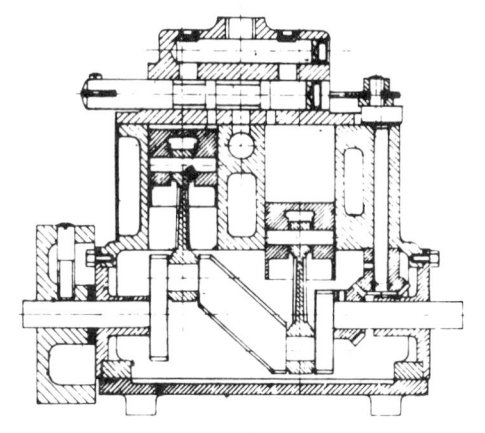

FIGURE 4.4
CROSS SECTION OF SUN ENGINE

arrangement. Since the two cylinders are single-acting, the pistons will be 180° out of phase, hence these twins are in effect a single double-acting engine.

One other asset possessed by the piston valve, which attracts some commercial interest, is the ease of quantity manufacture. Many components only require turning or boring and most continental manufacturers have made use of modern precision equipment to produce engines using simple piston valves. Many of these are in the toy category, so that if they have a short life and suffer from leakage, it is not considered worth doing anything to improve their design. In fact, since many are in the possession of youthful operators, some steam leakage no doubt adds to the owner's pleasure. For those who come into possession of such an engine, constant lubrication will help to eliminate some wear and keep leakage at bay. Even for the better class of engine, it is essential that proper attention is given to lubrication. It is not very practical to fit rings in really small piston valves and it does not take long to realise that movement of the valve back and forth in the valve chamber will cause wear on both bearing surfaces. In order to contain this, attention to lubrication is essential but some wear can be eliminated if the valve and the cylinder are made from dissimilar metals, so making for a good bearing combination. Reboring the chamber and replacing the valve is the only cure for leakage after a long period of use.

Engines used in high speed work generally have piston valves, and these engines are more often than not of the single cylinder, single-acting type, but in order to gain efficiency it is often the practice to have separate valves controlling the inlet and exhaust ports. Figure 4.5 shows such an engine which was described in 'Model Engineer', October 1943. The inlet is so arranged to act as a supplementary exhaust valve, for one thing that has to be borne in mind when designing a steam engine is to make sure of a free exhaust system. It is much easier to get the steam into the cylinder under pressure than to get it out at low or zero pressure after it has performed

39

Introducing Model Marine Steam

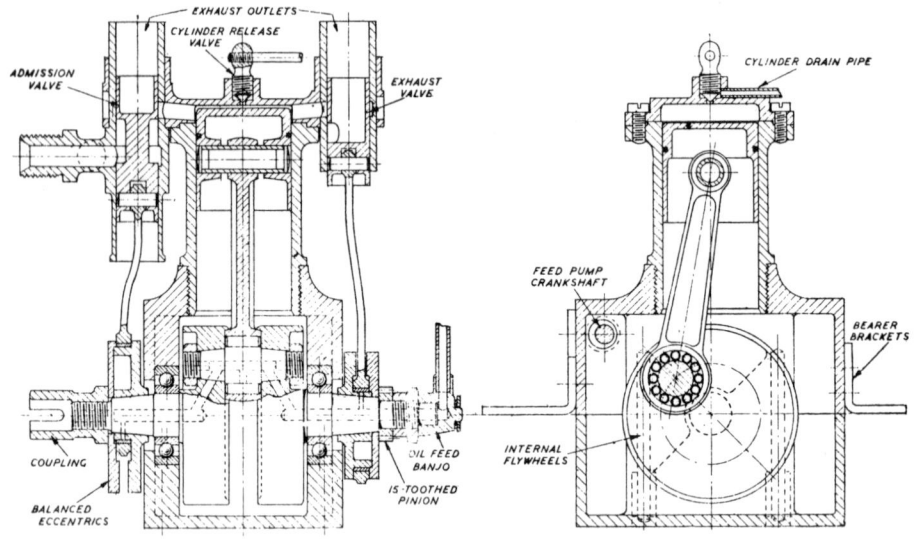

FIGURE 4.5

its work, and in high speed engines it is often necessary to take this course of action. Many engines depend on uniflow ports only for exhaust release, and if they are of the simple variety then back pressure will arise in the cylinder. It is much better to use uniflow ports as a supplement to the main exhaust port in attempts to improve performance.

POPPET VALVES

Many high-speed engines make use of poppet valves, following the methods of the internal combustion engine. Figure 4.6 shows a common layout where the valves are set at the side of the engine, but like the I/C engine, an overhead arrangement of the valves can be used. The valves are driven in the same manner as other poppet valve engines by cams which are gear or chain driven to give the required reduction in operating speeds in relation to the engine's crankshaft.

A point that has to be watched in the construction of poppet valves is the necessity of obtaining a good steam-tight seal between the valve and its face. This is an obvious requirement, but not so obvious is the need to maintain leak-tight fits on the valve spindles, perhaps not so important for the exhaust, but a leak here can cause problems within the boat. A steam-tight fit with freedom of movement is a definite requirement on the inlet valve spindle and in most cases this precludes, as on other types of engine, the use of a gland, hence retaining rings machined in the spindle are often used to maintain the seal.

Careful work is needed in shaping the cams and one disadvantage of using poppet valves in such a simple layout is that the points of admission, cut-off, and exhausting of the steam are fixed, whereas with other valves driven by some form of link motion some alteration to valve events can readily be made. In general, the cult of the high speed en-

Piston and other Valves

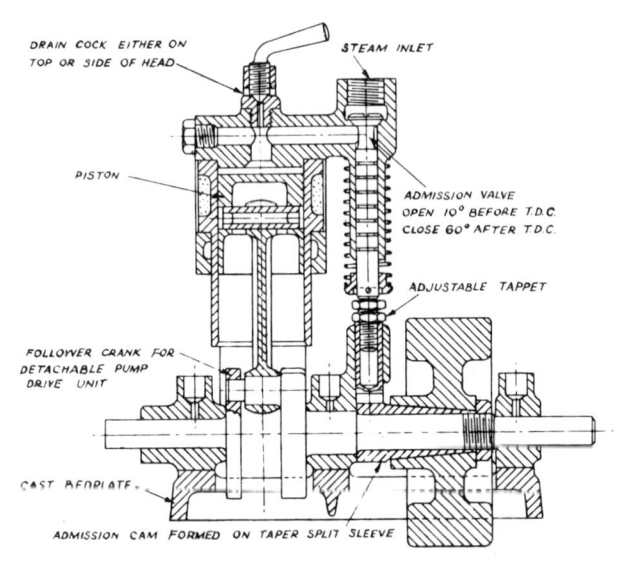

FIGURE 4.6 CROSS SECTION OF SPARTAN HIGH SPEED UNIFLOW ENGINE

gine means that followers intend to use the engine in racing hydroplanes, and this becomes a fetish to the dedicated minority. If the reader has inclinations in this direction, then a voluntary apprenticeship with the simpler types of engine is well advised in order to gain experience.

CLAPPER VALVES

In the quest for high speed, experiments have been made in the use of engines having valves in the cylinder head tripped by a projection on the top of the piston, figure 4.7. The principle is in common use in model aeroplanes where CO_2 gas is the power source, and while the system on first sight may not seem to be an efficient one, it does work well. As the piston rises in the cylinder, the spigot formed on the top of the piston lifts the valve, shown here as a plain ball, but in high-speed engines a more sophisticated form of valve is used.

Steam is admitted and the piston is driven down, being forced back over top dead centre by inertia stored in the flywheel. At the end of the power stroke

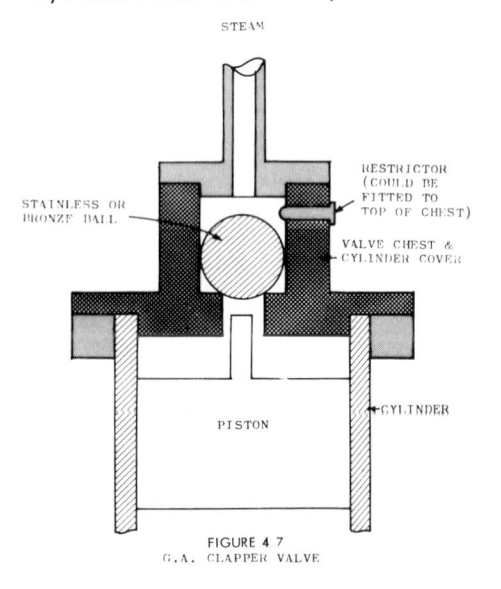

FIGURE 4.7 G.A. CLAPPER VALVE

41

Introducing Model Marine Steam

steam is exhausted through the uniflow ports and on the return stroke, what little steam is left in the cylinder is compressed and provides a cushioning effect on the piston.

These 'knocker' or 'clapper' valve engines have to be turned over by hand in the direction of desired rotation, and the larger ones will require the use of a starter cord and pulley on the shaft, as for an internal combustion engine. They will rotate in either direction according to the starting mode. In the past, most of these engines have been used for racing hydroplanes, but there seems to be no reason why smaller ones should not prove satisfactory for use in slower running craft. In the model aeroplane world their use has generally been in the smaller sizes and they function quite well. It would seem that there is room for experiment here, especially for the man who runs straight course boats, and associated with a low pressure flash steam boiler it could well provide a simple, easily made outfit.

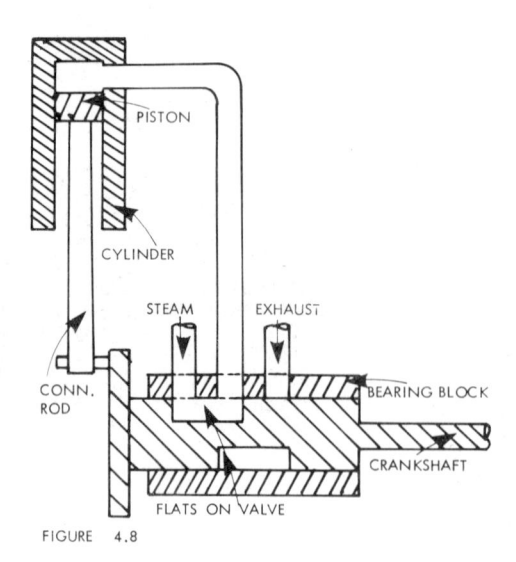

ROTARY VALVES

In an effort to make the steam engine simpler in construction, many designs have been prepared to use the crankshaft as a rotary valve. Figure 4.8 illustrates just one example of this type, where the inlet and exhausting of steam are controlled by flats machined on the crankshaft, which as it turns allows steam into or out of the cylinder. On the face of it, this would seem to be an easy way to control the steam, but like the piston valve, wear is the enemy of such a system and perhaps more so as such an engine needs to have a good fitting crank in its bearings, ideally with no clearance which unfortunately will not allow for good running. The two requirements, i.e. free running and steam tightness, conflict, with the result that wear takes over and leakage occurs. If such a design is considered then the designer needs to increase the diameter of the crank and make sure that lubrication is at its best, preferably pressurised.

TURBINES

While clapper, poppet, piston and other types of valves have all been used in the development of the high speed engine, the high efficiency turbine of big ships has been consistently ignored by the small scale marine engineer and the few attempts made at following full-size designs have all proved to be notoriously inefficient in small scale.

Most of the attempts made at building small turbines, except for the few mentioned before, have, it must be admitted, generally used rotors cut from discs of sheet metal, with blades formed by bending or being soldered on to the rotor. In effect they are not much more

Opposite, Fig. 4-9, a modern steam turbine from Japan.

FIGURE 4.8

Piston and other Valves

Introducing Model Marine Steam

than fans blown round by the steam, the whole design being not far removed from Hero's steam engine of the Ancient Greeks.

It is not the authors' intention to delve into the techniques of steam turbine design, for at the present time they are not qualified to do so, and at this stage of their writing it is suggested that this again is a field where the lover of innovation and experiment could venture. Notwithstanding the difficulties, this could prove most exciting and rewarding for the experimenter who is not in a hurry for results, or who seeks fame, for he must be ready for many a failure in his quest for success.

Generally marine engines have made use of the slide or piston valves to control the in and out flow of steam to the cylinders, but there has been a large number of designs of other types of valve used in an endeavour to improve efficiency. Many of these would be considered unsuitable for use in the model marine engineer's engine room for a variety of reasons, but mainly because of the complexity of the parts involved, and especially in connection with the associated valve gear, which nearly always seemed to be rather complicated. Another factor which precludes the use of some sophisticated valves and associated gears is that they derived much of their efficiency from their large size and comparatively slow movement. Two such types of valves and gears were in use for many years on Mississippi sternwheelers, and used poppet valves that were lifted off their seatings to admit or release steam from the cylinders. They were driven by either a cam on the main shaft in the Rees cut-off or by eccentrics in the California cut-off.

These and similar engines were claimed to be more efficient than comparable locomotive types, but it is suspected that if they were worked at a higher speed than was usual with river boats (30 revs/min) then the inertia of the various parts would soon cancel out any advantage gained. Except for the dyed-in-the-wool enthusiast, such engines can be eliminated as possible subjects for our miniature marine fleet.

Poppet valves, however, have been used successfully in small engines; they are particularly useful in high revving non-reversing engines, and one good example is the *Spartan* high-speed engine designed by Edgar T. Westbury, figure 4.6. It will be seen that the admission valve is similar to that used on the much more common internal combustion engine. Controlled by a cam, it lifts off its seating to admit steam to the cylinder. Note the series of oil retaining rings turned in the valve spindle to maintain steam tightness. Exhaust is taken care of by uniflow ports drilled in the cylinder walls, just above where the piston reaches bottom dead centre, and is taken away to the exhaust pipe by a collector ring. Poppet valves can be used to control the exhaust as well as inlet steam. All that is required is another cam driven valve, set to exhaust at the right moment.

Care needs to be taken in the choice of suitable materials, particularly in high speed engines operating at high temperature. There will be quite a lot of pounding on valve faces, control springs need to be right to eliminate valve bounce, and most important of all, the angle of valve and valve face must agree. Valves have in fact to be ground in as is done with I/C engines.

Chapter Five

Other Engine Developments

In Chapter 4, steam engine development due to improved valve arrangements was dealt with, but the variations in valve arrangements are not the only means by which engines can be improved in efficiency, and of course, there is always the problem of getting the engine into the allotted space. Sometimes these two problems coincide in their solution. Usually, though, the model marine man is not so much interested in thermal efficiency as with the problem of space, and therefore in this chapter both these subjects will be dealt with, albeit in outline, for there is insufficient room between the covers of such a book as this to deal in detail with all the configurations and developments available.

COMPOUNDING

From the earliest days of maritime steam the designer of full-sized craft has had the problem of stowing sufficient fuel for the steamer's passage, and various ways of increasing efficiency were tried, such as new valve gear layouts, better boilers and one method which has survived, the art of compounding. Compounding is a system where the exhaust steam from one cylinder is passed into another so that further useful energy can be extracted from the steam at a lower pressure. Figure 5.1 shows a simple layout for compound engines; as will be seen, the steam first passes into the normal steam chest and after being used at the initial pressure (which is usually higher than it would be in a single cylinder engine) it is exhausted into the inlet side of a second cylinder. After working this cylinder, the steam remaining is finally exhausted in the normal fashion.

In the model world it is uncommon for a compound to be used, and more often a twin cylinder engine with both cylinders of the same size (figure 5.2) such as the Stuart Double 10 or the Reeves *Warrior* is favoured. The advantage of double cylinder engines is, of course, the absence of a dead point, hence they are self-starting, whereas the compound must be treated as a single cylinder engine. In full size practice the compound has to be turned over dead centres in order to start. This is done either with a bar in the flywheel, or on big engines with a separate 'barring' engine. Alternatively, a so called 'simpling valve' is fitted so that steam at boiler pressure is admitted to the low pressure cylinder on starting. In effect it becomes a twin cylinder engine with unequal sized cylinders. A good example of a compound is seen in the Stuart Turner range where the traditional open column method con-

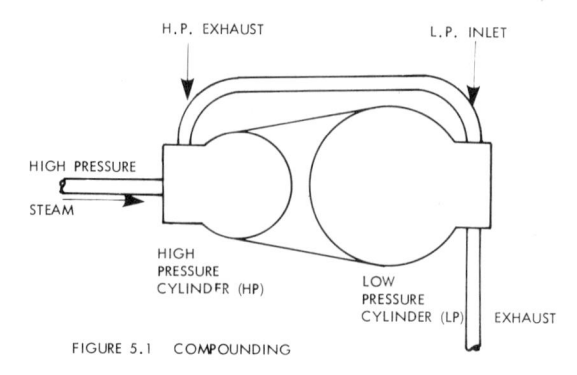

Introducing Model Marine Steam

FIGURE 5.1 COMPOUNDING

struction is common to both a compound and a twin cylinder engine. With the exception of the cylinder block, identical components are used.

TRIPLE EXPANSION

A further development of the compound engine was the triple expansion engine, which, as its name signifies, makes use of three expansions of the steam in order to increase thermal efficiency, figure 5.3. Triple expansion engines are popular with amateurs and the Stuart example is to be found in many scale models, so faithfully copying prototype engine rooms. Many more triples are built as exhibition models in their own right and can be seen at most model engineering displays. By the time steam reaches the third cylinder it has very little energy left, and it is general practice in full size operation to introduce a degree of re-heating between the different stages of expansion. More important perhaps is the fact that all triples should finally exhaust their steam into a condenser, which in conjunction with a vacuum pump effectively reduces back pressure on the piston of the final stage, so increasing efficiency still further.

Sometimes, instead of a large low pressure cylinder, the engine is provided with two smaller ones. These operate in parallel and obtain the same result as a large cylinder, but with the advantage of smaller components. It has been known for a further stage of expansion to be tried in large engines making for quadruple expansion, but so far as the writers know this has not been tried as a working proposition in the model world.

TANDEM COMPOUNDS

In engine rooms where space is very much at a premium, e.g. small coasters,

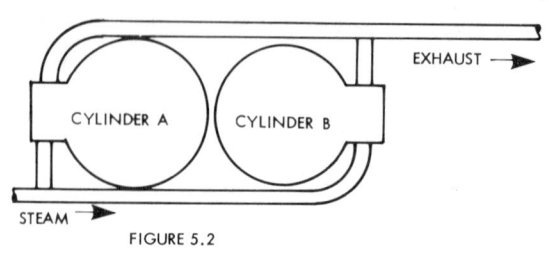

FIGURE 5.2

Other Engine Developments

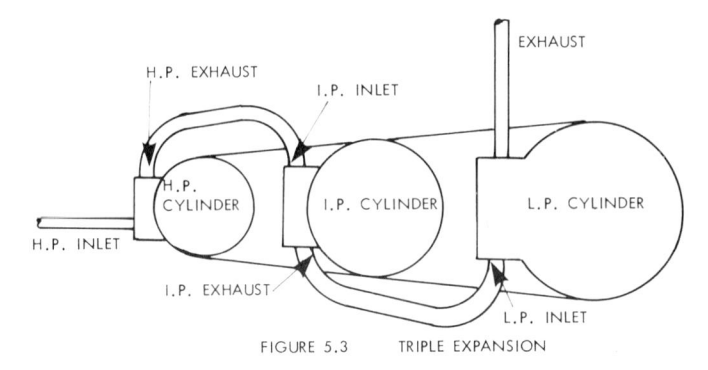

FIGURE 5.3 TRIPLE EXPANSION

puffers etc., compound engines are fitted, but unlike the general run, instead of having cylinders side by side they are fitted one above the other in tandem fashion, figure 5.4. Common piston and valve rods are used and the exhaust from the HP cylinder is arranged to exhaust into the LP steam chest, as in any other compound. While not often seen in miniature this type of engine would prove a challenge to a model engineer, for among other problems associated with something out of the ordinary, there is the problem of providing a double steam-tight gland between the cylinders.

CONDENSERS

Condensing of the exhaust steam to reduce back pressure will always theoretically increase thermal efficiency, although in our small engines this advantage is dubious; however, in the desire to obtain a faithful copy of the prototype the installation of a condenser, sometimes by a dummy but better still a working replica, is essential.

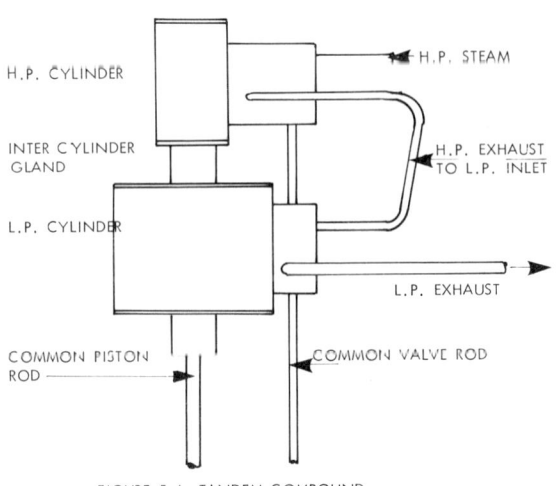

FIGURE 5.4 TANDEM COMPOUND

47

Introducing Model Marine Steam

Of course for an engine that will never grace a steamer's engine room but which is to remain a showpiece, a condenser adds to the charm and correctness of the final product. The simplest form of condenser is obtained by arranging the exhaust to pass through the hull and along the under part of the hull so that lake water acts as the coolant. Tubes are often used in parallel either side of or indeed forming parts of the keel and the 'keel' type of condenser has the advantage of not requiring a pumped water supply. It does of course suffer from the possibility of damage. More sophisticated condensers consist of a stack of pipes through which the exhaust steam is passed and which are in turn placed in a stream of cold water pumped from the outside. Figure 5.5 illustrates the principle and it should be noted that the process is sometimes reversed with steam passing through the main chamber and water via the tubes. The resulting condensate can be used in the boiler feed and in prototype operations this was a vital factor in improving efficiency as it reduced the amount of fresh water that had to be carried. For model work though, it can cause problems inasmuch as pumping hot water can occasionally cause difficulties. This should not deter those who strive after realism, however.

With all forms of compounding it is advantageous to operate the engine at a higher initial pressure that with a straight steam system. As stated before, the steam engine is obviously a heat engine and as such the higher the temperature it can be operated at the better. With ordinary engines a high boiler pressure could mean that exhaust pressure would also be high, hence energy would be wasted, but the reuse in the compound means that the maximum heat energy extraction takes place. This higher operating pressure means increased attention has to be paid to joints in the steam supply line and higher test pressures are necessary on the boiler. For normal simple working, a pressure of 40lbs/sq.in. is often found satisfactory, but with compound or triple expansion working, twice or three times this pressure is often used.

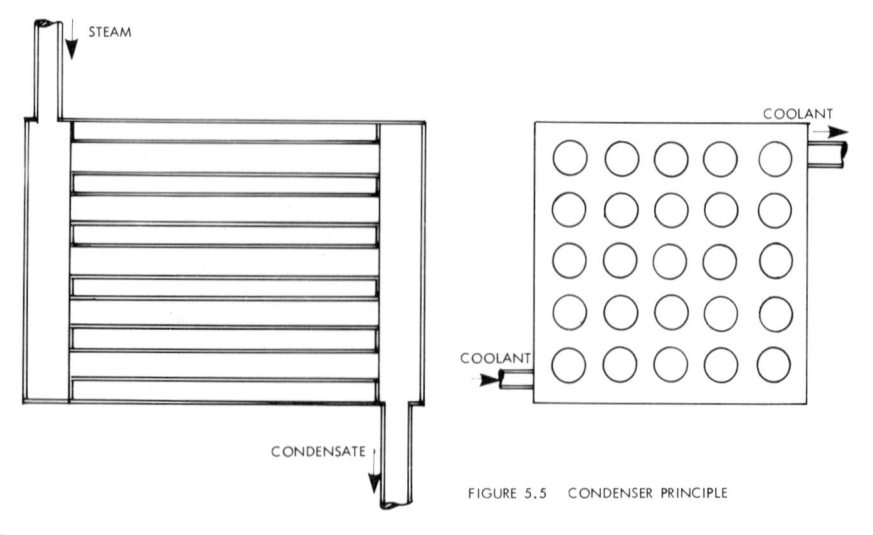

FIGURE 5.5 CONDENSER PRINCIPLE

Other Engine Developments

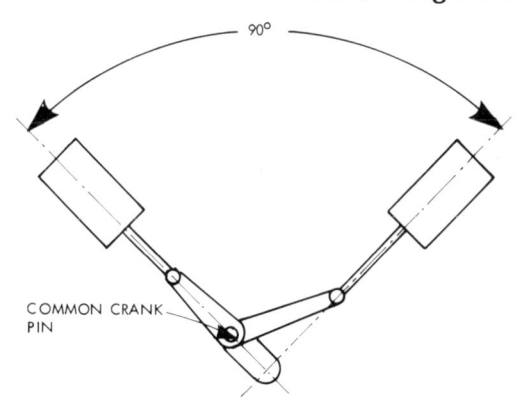

FIGURE 5.6 VEE FORMATION ARRANGEMENT

OTHER ENGINE TYPES

While compounding increases the efficiency of the steam engine, in model work other considerations take precedence over this, and quite often the more efficient use of the space available in the hull becomes a major point. Most power rooms make use of the engine in a vertical manner but when space is at a premium then a vee arrangement as in figure 5.6 is worth consideration, especially as the overall length can be almost halved by using it. Both pistons can act on the same crank pin, thus eliminating the need to make a two-throw crank, and both slide valves operate from a common set of eccentrics, figure 5.7

HORIZONTAL ENGINES

The use of horizontal engines has been previously mentioned and for those building light launch type boats, an Edgar T. Westbury design, the *Cygnet*, is a suitable one for boats up to about 36in. overall. This has the added advantage of not requiring any castings as it is designed to be machined from stock materials. Full details are shown on M.A.P. plan No. M.13. While Edgar

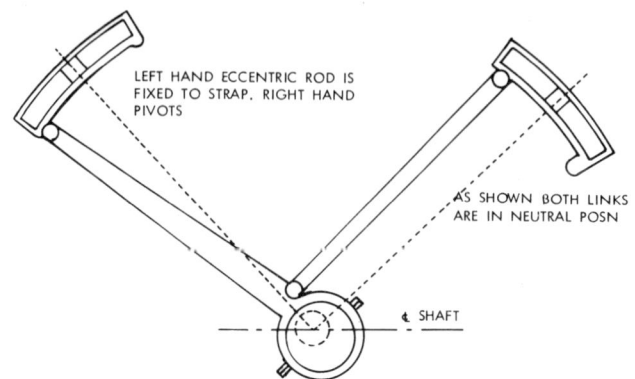

FIGURE 5.7 DRAWN WITH GEAR IN CENTRE POSITION

49

Introducing Model Marine Steam

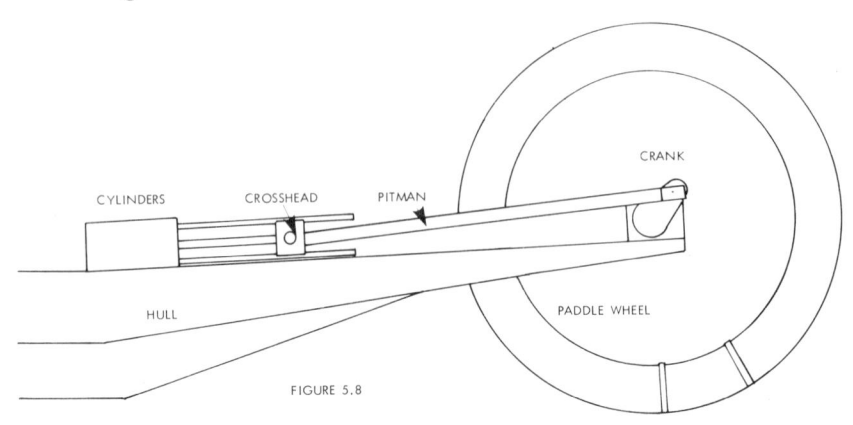

FIGURE 5.8

[Diagram labels: CYLINDERS, CROSSHEAD, PITMAN, CRANK, HULL, PADDLE WHEEL]

Westbury was better known for his internal combustion engine designs he did produce several drawings for steam plants, including the diagonal paddle engine complete with feathering paddles mentioned at the end of this chapter.

For those who require a horizontal engine that can be obtained ready to assemble, then the Stuart Turner *Score* may provide a suitable machine for their use.

With such a long history behind it, the variations of the theme that have been

A Championship cup winning model at the 1978 Model Engineer Exhibition, a 1/12th scale stern wheel paddle engine built by G. E. Hartung.

Other Engine Developments

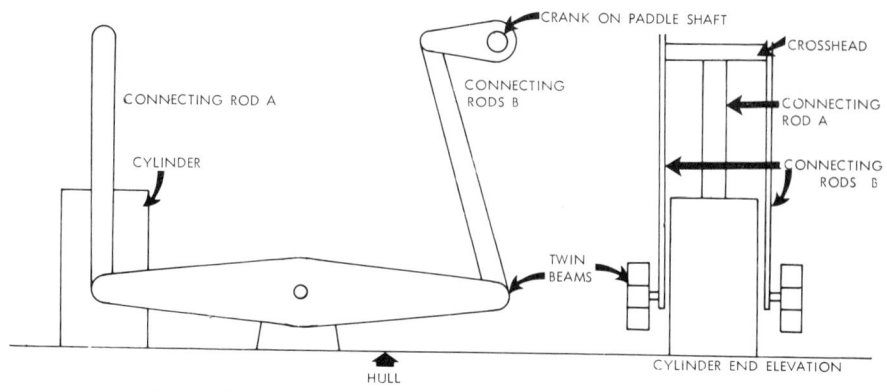

FIGURE 5.9 SIDE LEVER ENGINE — DIAGRAMMATIC ONLY

(Labels: CONNECTING ROD A, CYLINDER, CRANK ON PADDLE SHAFT, CONNECTING RODS B, TWIN BEAMS, HULL, CROSSHEAD, CONNECTING ROD A, CONNECTING RODS B, CYLINDER END ELEVATION)

applied to the steam engine are too numerous to be mentioned in these pages, but once interest has been generated, the builder of miniature steam plants will probably begin inquiring into other forms of layouts of engines, and while this may prove interesting, before one embarks on the construction of an unusual type of engine, it is as well to ask the question, 'Why was it not found useful or popular in full-size practice?'. Fantastic claims have been made for many types of engine, but in practice there have usually been some very good reasons for their non-acceptance.

One other arrangement not often seen in models but used extensively on Mississippi sternwheel steam boats is illustrated in outline in figure 5.8. This has the advantage of eliminating many of the drive problems for the rear paddle wheel is driven in the style of an outside-cylindered locomotive with cranks on the paddle shaft. Valve gears on these boats were complicated affairs and any prospective builders are advised to steer clear of reproducing them in miniature unless the scale used is a big one. It would be better to settle for a more common gear, Joy's being a suggested suitable choice.

BEAM ENGINES

Beam engines have been used to propel steam boats and were mainly one of two patterns, the more common one in the UK being the side lever beam engine, and these make nice out-of-the-ordinary models. While full size engines were ornate and full of detail, model copies can be much simplified while still maintaining the charm of the original (figure 5.9). On the North American continent, beam engines with the conventional overhead beam were often used, as shown in figure 5.10. This use of the beam engine gave rise to the term 'Walking Beam' as indeed the beam does walk with the ship.

DIAGONAL ENGINES

In order to accommodate paddle steamer engines in as economical a space as possible, they were often arranged in diagonal form. This was the type of engine that survived until the last days of the paddle steamer and there are many who can remember the sight of such engines in operation, for it was the thing to have the engines on full view to the passengers, who could enjoy the

51

Introducing Model Marine Steam

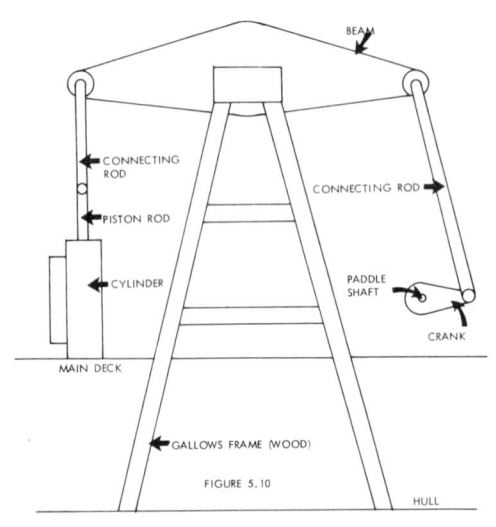

FIGURE 5.10

sight, sound and also the smell of live steam in action. In the model field one design that has often been used is from the drawing board of Edgar Westbury, and like his other designs, it is obtainable from M.A.P. Plans Service, numbered M.9. The diagonal form is clear in figure 5.11.

Fig.5·11 Diagonal paddle steamer engine built to a design by the late Edgar Westbury.

52

Chapter Six

Firetube Boilers

The domestic kettle is well known as a producer of wet steam, for that is all that is required of it, i.e. the capacity to raise water to boiling point, which under normal atmospheric conditions is 100° centigrade, a temperature which satisfies most household requirements. This most common of boilers is not an efficient machine since a lot of the available heat is lost around the sides, and in an attempt to improve the efficiency and the performance, so-called quick boiling kettles were common at one time. These had a number of tubes passing through the base and sides, figure 6.1, which increased the water area subjected to heat, so decreasing the time and amount of heat required to reach boiling point.

The resulting commonplace object was in effect a firetube boiler, and is the principle used in rather more sophisticated designs intended for raising steam to higher temperatures and pressures than needed for making a cup of 'engineer's friend'. In model work it is an easy matter to improve the simple pot boiler described in Chapter 2 by incorporating fire tubes into the design as shown in figure 6.2. Four parallel rows of holes are drilled in the boiler shell and short pieces of tube are silver-soldered into place. With the boiler mounted in a casing lined with asbestos or some other fireproof material, the efficiency is raised, faster steaming is achieved, and a larger engine can be steamed than would otherwise be the case with a simple pot boiler. Furthermore, if coupled with an efficient burner, even more demanding engines can be accommodated.

If the boat into which the power plant is to be installed is a river launch, perhaps of the *African Queen* type, then a vertical boiler would be appropriate and firetube boilers are most suitable for use in this form. Figure 6.3 shows diagrammatically a simple arrangement of a vertical firetube boiler. The only difficult piece of construction is in forming the top plates of the boiler and the firebox, as they will need flanges where joining with the side wall and flue. The art of flanging plates is not too difficult and with care and patience the job should be within the capabilities of everyone. The most important thing to

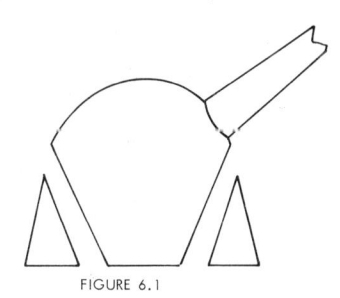

FIGURE 6.1

Introducing Model Marine Steam

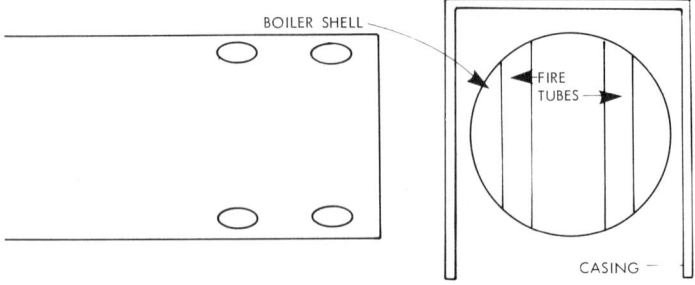

FIGURE 6.2

bear in mind during these operations is to soften the copper repeatedly by heating to a bright red and dropping it into water. Working the copper makes it hard and if worked too long without annealing (softening) it becomes brittle and can fracture.

The boiler shown in figure 6.3 has only the centre flue to provide heating surface outside the firebox. Although in this type of steam generator there is quite a lot of heating surface contained in the firebox itself, since the object is to gain as much heating surface as possible, the development in figure 6.4 is well worth while. The top plate of the boiler has been lowered and both this and the firebox plate are drilled with holes through which tubes are silver soldered in place. The chimney flue is now fixed to a removable cover plate and the gap between this and the boiler

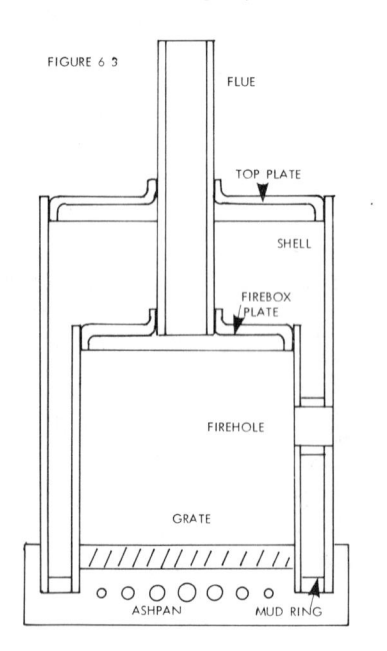

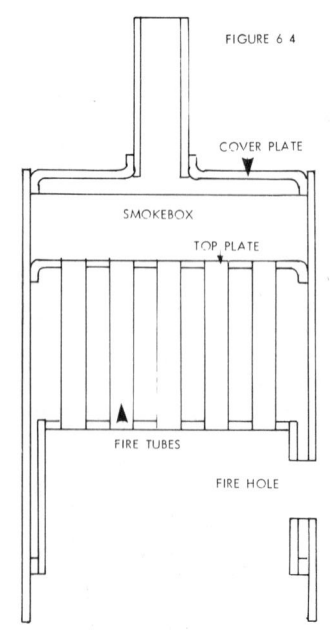

Firetube boilers

top forms a smokebox. Increased heating surface makes the additional work of building a multi-tubular boiler worth the effort.

Vertical boilers lend themselves to firing by many differing kinds of fuel including solid ones such as wood or coal. All vertical boilers need mounting in such a fashion as to allow a free flow of air to the firebox, and usually this is achieved by fixing a perforated ring of metal to the base of the boiler. The perforations can be enlarged or blanked off to suit the air supply needs of the burner, and their size will be determined by adjustment in use. With solid fuels, some means of hand-feeding the fuel to the firebox must be provided, usually a short tube joining coincidental holes in the boiler shell and the inner firebox, and fitted with a swing door and catch on the outside as in the prototype. Alternatively, firing can be done in the same way as old-time Sentinel steam wagons, via a vertical tube running from the smokebox top through the top plate, again fitted with a door as in the full size example, figure 6.5.

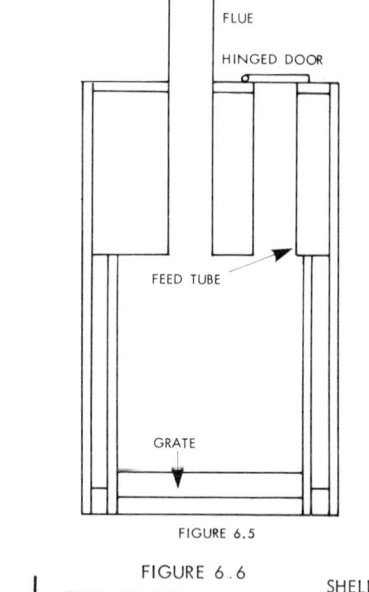

The commonest form of model marine boiler is the centre flue type, shown sectionally in figure 6.6. Essentially we have a simple pot type boiler, but instead of applying heat to the outside, a centre flue has been introduced, through which the heat, generally supplied from some form of blow-torch, is directed. In this basic design much heat is lost and invariably water tubes are fitted through the centre flue, figure 6.7, and the efficiency of the

FIGURE 6.5

FIGURE 6.6

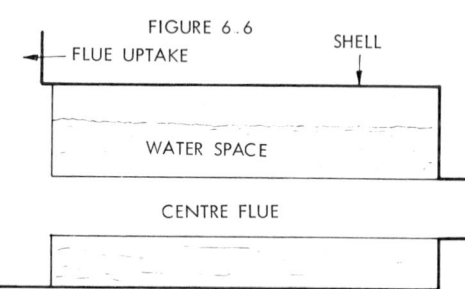

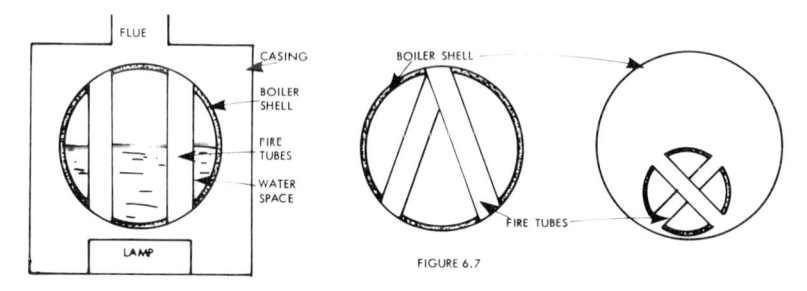

FIGURE 6.7

Introducing Model Marine Steam

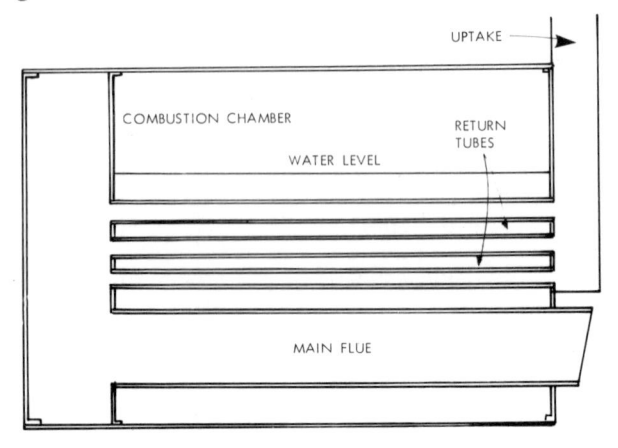

FIGURE 6.8

boiler is raised because of the increased surface area offered to the flame. In effect we have made the boiler into a hybrid with both fire and water tubes. The tubes can be arranged in various ways; parallel rows of tubes, or in a rotating pattern, starting vertical and each successive tube being slightly angled in relation to the previous one, or in a fashion whereby each tube is at 90° to the previous one. You 'pays your money and takes your choice' but remember that whatever arrangement is adopted the gases must have a clear flow, as back pressure from the flue will often cause a blowlamp to go out.

Centre flue boilers are very reliable and like most horizontal boilers have the advantage of low centre of gravity combined with a reasonable water capacity, the last being very comforting to have if operating on large open waters, for a lamp failure way out on an open lake can be frustrating if there is not sufficient capacity of reserve steam to get the boat back to land.

Another efficient design of firetube boiler is the return tube type of which there are several varieties, the most popular in small work being the 'Scotch dry back' shown diagrammatically in figure 6.8. As can be seen, the hot gases are first directed through the main flue and on reaching the end of the boiler they are re-directed back through another series of tubes, eventually entering the smokebox and the uptake to discharge to atmosphere. The great advantage of a return tube boiler over other types is its greatly reduced overall length, making it popular in full size practice for use in such boats as small coasters of the 'puffer' type. All types of fuel can be used in these boilers, but with solid fuel the main flue is enlarged and a grate and ashpan fitted. The dry back type of return tube boiler is fitted with a removable end to the combustion chamber, allowing access to the tubes for cleaning, a very necessary facility if used for solid fuel.

Increased heating surface is gained in a wet back type of return tube boiler, figure 6.9, because the combustion chamber as well as the tubes is surrounded by water. In spite of the aforementioned advantage, this type is not always recommended because of

Firetube Boilers

the obvious difficulty that arises in guaranteeing a leak-free assembly, plus the problem of correcting any leaks that may develop in service.

While all the designs illustrated by the sketches show only one main flue, this is not always the case. In most model installations a single flue suffices but in prototype designs, multiple flues and furnaces are commonplace. There is a lot to be said for the use of more than one burner in miniature marine works, particularly when the boat is a large one, and the use of multiple flues can remove the need for additional boiler(s).

Shallow draft boats all over the world have favoured the use of a type of boiler that has not found many followers in our hobby. This is the 'locomotive' boiler, shown in figure 6.10, and the section will be readily recognised by those who know the steam locomotive. Most suited to solid fuels, although a large proportion of the prototypes both on land and water used oil, the loco boiler has the advantage of a good reserve capacity, and compared with many other types, is relatively efficient. Fuel is burnt in a firebox at one end and the products of combustion travel through firetubes to the smokebox, thence to the atmosphere. In small practice the rows of firetubes incorporate two or three larger tubes through which the steam supply tubes are looped in order to superheat the steam.

The locomotive type boiler shown in figure 6.10 is typical of those used in their thousands by the live steam locomotive fraternity, and since its use has proved satisfactory it can be recommended as a working propositon for marine use. Water is contained in the spaces above and along the sides and back and front of the firebox, and since water separates the inner firebox from the backhead, the type is generally termed a 'wetback'. Some simplification, making use of castings for the backhead is shown in figure 6.11, and

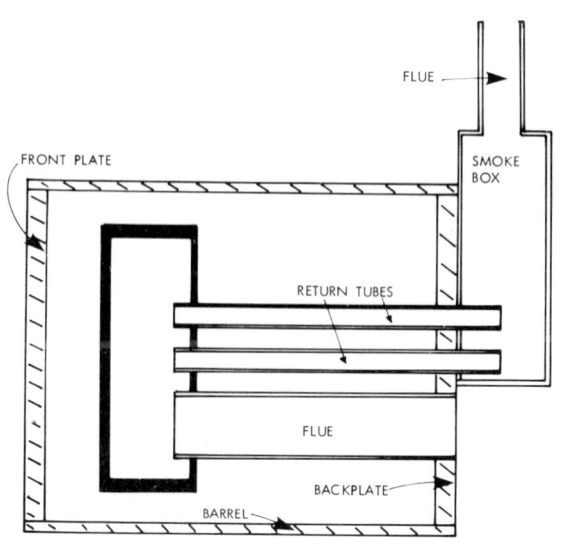

FIGURE 6.9   WET BACK RETURN TUBE BOILER

57

Introducing Model Marine Steam

here the backhead forms part of the firebox. With no water separating the backhead from the furnace, this feature is not unexpectedly known as a 'dryback'. The design was common up to the mid 1920s, when it died out in England, and the amateur favoured the wetback that is so common today. In some respects the dryback is easier to make but of course it loses some thermal efficiency and has the disadvantage of having castings as part of the boiler, a design feature that is not looked upon with favour; however, as long as the materials and workmanship are top grade, the arrangement should prove satisfactory.

A marine modification of the loco boiler popular in some quarters and particularly for use with solid fuel, although both oil and gas could be used for firing, is depicted in figure 6.12. With the exception of the end plates all other parts are tubes, the strongest form of construction, and if the four plates are formed well and care is taken in their jointing, this type of boiler can prove one of the best. If this boiler is to be used with solid fuel, it is quite practical to arrange that the grate and ashpan can be withdrawn as one unit from the end of the boiler.

SUPERHEATING

Since the object of heating water is to generate steam, it behoves us to ensure that the steam offered to the engine shall be as hot as possible. The steam engine is of course, a heat engine, and the more heat that can be applied the more effective the machine will be. Of course, any droplets of water that are present in the steam need to be eliminated, and to do this after steam leaves the boiler additional heating is applied. In addition to this drying of the steam, most engine designs expect that the steam reaching the steam chest will be more than dry steam, and so additional heat is applied, causing superheating. Superheated steam is accepted as a common factor today and will make the difference between an indifferently performing engine and one with a sparkle in its action, so particular attention should be given to providing enough superheat. In a firetube boiler the obvious way is to take the steam feed through the flue so that it passes through the furnace flame, and in the case of the locomotive type boiler two or three of the fire tubes are enlarged to accommodate 'U' shaped superheater tubes which are inserted from the smokebox end. These will carry

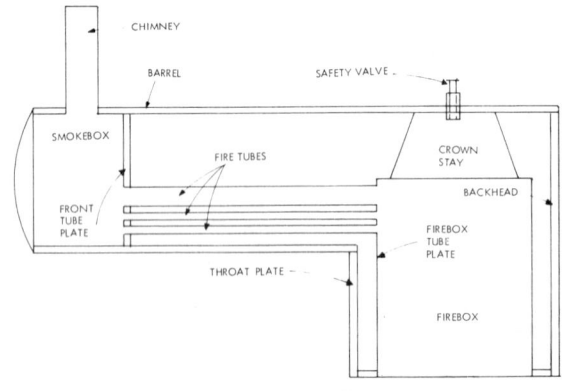

FIGURE 6.10   LOCOMOTIVE TYPE BOILER

Firetube Boilers

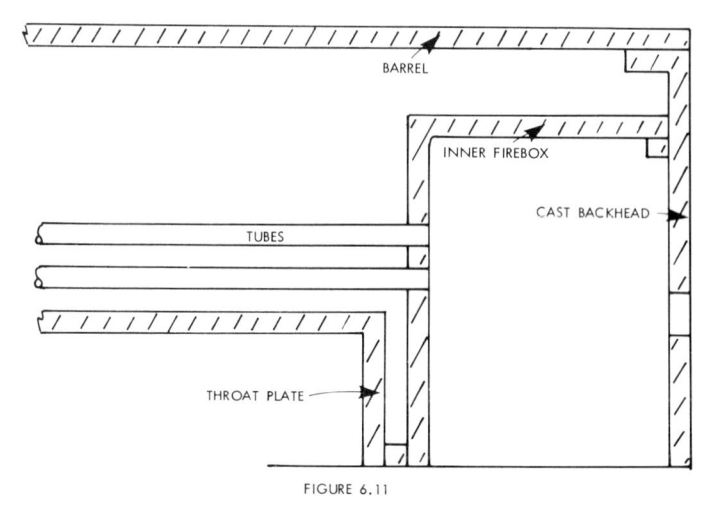

FIGURE 6.11

the steam feed right down to the firebox. Unless special arrangements are made, the bend of the tube usually lines up with the end of the flues and quite often is formed from a solid block of copper, figure 6.13. Some builders use stainless steel tube for superheater tubes and in the case of the loco type boilers take the element right to the firebox, but for marine work this is not necessary. It is sometimes arranged that the steam feed is taken from the boiler through the superheater before reaching a control valve, and this has the advantage of

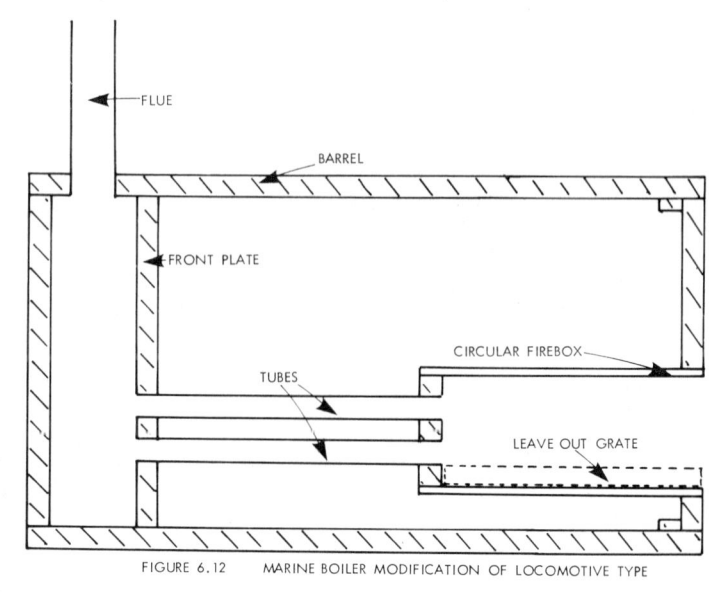

FIGURE 6.12   MARINE BOILER MODIFICATION OF LOCOMOTIVE TYPE

59

Introducing Model Marine Steam

TUBES

SUPERHEATER FLUE

SUPERHEATER FLUE

TUBES

COPPER BLOCK BRAZED TO TUBES

FIGURE 6.13

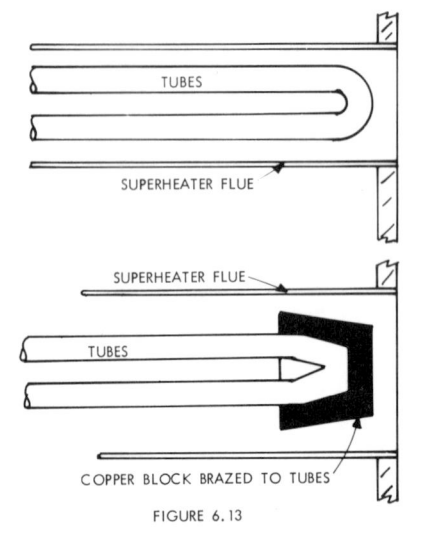

keeping the superheater full of steam. Generally though, steam is taken from the highest point of the boiler via a screw-down valve fitted in a bush in the boiler barrel.

The pressures required for general use in marine steam plants are only moderate and it is not likely that the relatively high pressures, 90 lbs/sq. in. allied with very high superheat as used by our locomotive contemporaries, will be used. If, in fact, high pressures are required to give satisfaction in the average steam model, then it is worth examining the engine to see what improvements can be made there, rather than to work a boat at extra high pressure. Many a well-running model is to be seen with an operating boiler pressure below 60 lbs/sq.in.

MAP plan Inchcolm, a Clyde puffer 24¾ ins long by 7 ins beam, is just large enough to take a small boiler and oscillating engine.

Chapter Seven

Watertube Boilers

While, as seen in Chapter 6, the use of firetubes in boilers will increase their efficiency, there are other ways of achieving the same object, and one of the simplest is to insert a number of rods (rivets) in the barrel so that they resemble a hedgehog on the underneath, figure 7.1. By so doing the heating surface is increased, but rather than take this trouble it is just as easy to replace these rods with water tubes similar to the simple arrangement of figure 7.2. Indeed, this is the commonest way of improving the pot boiler, and many designs using such an arrangement are only one step removed from toy type boilers. If the tubes are given a slope as shown in the drawing, circulation is improved and better use is made of the heat applied to the boiler. It will be noted that the whole of the boiler is enclosed in a casing, and when using water tubes, this is an essential design point that will much help the boiler to prove satisfactory in steam generation. Also, in all live steam work it is essential that all exposed pipes should be lagged; after all, it is not much use making sure that the steam produced is really hot if some of the heat is going to be lost to the open air.

YARROW BOILERS

The large steam ships of the merchant and naval fleets almost invariably use some form of water tube boiler, so in our small editions we are following in some very good footsteps. One of the types of marine water tube boiler that has been used extensively is the 'Yarrow'. Bearing the name of one of the most famous of British shipbuilders, the type was found on many a ship on the high seas, and although not so often modelled, it can prove satisfactory for model boat steam raising, and in addition will give the model marine engineer a correct replica

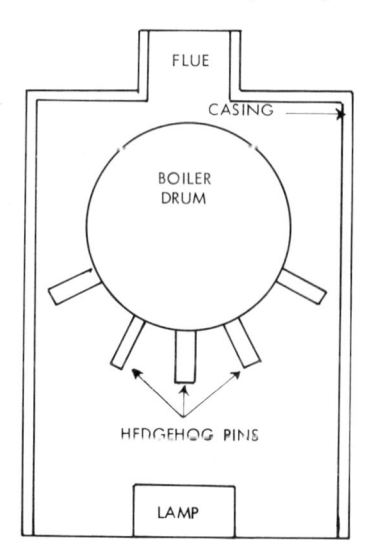

FIGURE 7.1 END SECTION ONLY

Introducing Model Marine Steam

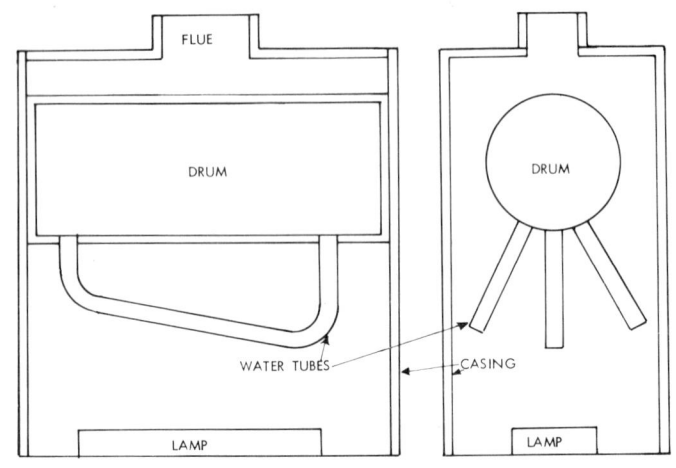

FIGURE 7.2 ONLY ONE WATER TUBE SHOWN IN SIDE SECTION

for his boiler room, figure 7.3. Essentially, the Yarrow has three main components, a water and steam drum and two bottom headers, the three items being situated at the corners of a triangle connected with large downcoming tubes outside the boiler casing at each end, and, within the casing, by a number of water tubes in the furnace area. Water circulates from the drum through the end downcomers, along the bottom headers and up the water tubes by convection as the tubes are heated. Heat is kept within the lined casing and as the downcomers are outside the furnace, it is necessary to lag them to retain heat. Even though circulation is by convection currents, we only require a small difference in temperature between the downcomer and the water tubes to maintain the flow. With the Yarrow it could be advantageous to feed water

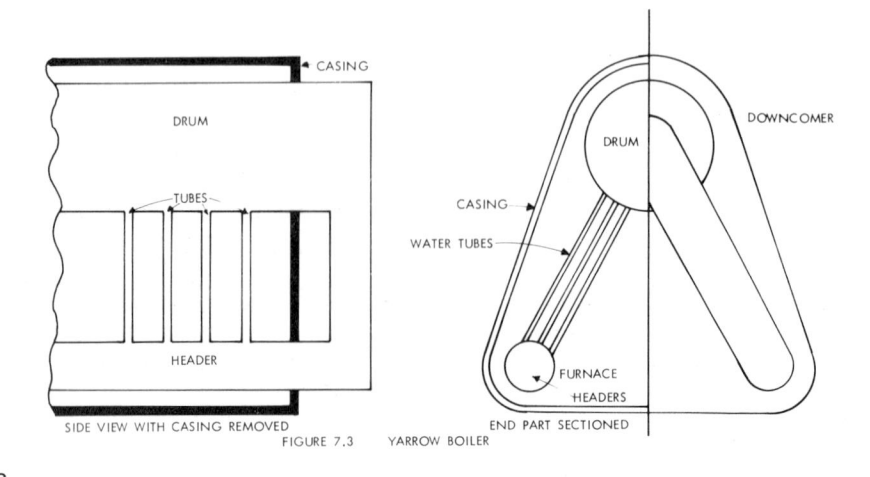

FIGURE 7.3 YARROW BOILER

Watertube Boilers

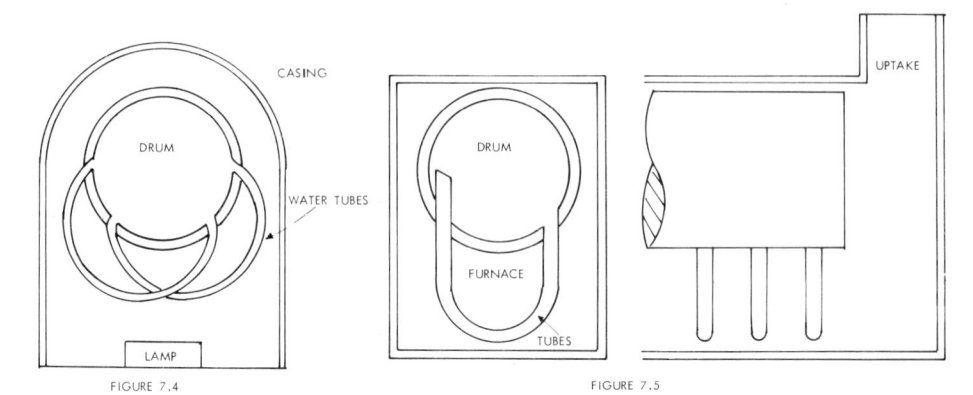

FIGURE 7.4

FIGURE 7.5

into the boiler via the bottom headers in order to improve the flow and increase the temperature in the steam drum. This type of boiler is suitable for use with solid, liquid or gaseous fuels.

Although for simplicity the diagram only shows water tubes in rows of three, which incidentally is quite a usual arrangement, there is no reason, assuming the boiler is big enough, why the number or rows and the number of tubes in each row should not be increased in number. Some builders have arranged the tubes in each row in an angled fashion but the straightforward arrangement as shown works satisfactorily. With most water tube boilers the overall height compared with a centre flue is greater, but some saving in length is usually there to compensate for this. Water tube boilers are also built to carry a higher pressure than firetube designs, and thus are very suitable for use when a compound or triple expansion engine is to be the power unit. In this respect, a Yarrow in conjunction with such engines will be in line with the practice of many merchant ships, and for warships of the reciprocating engine era, they were a common sight in the Royal Navy's engine and boiler rooms.

SCOTT BOILERS

A logical development of the simple boiler of figure 7.2 was the Scott, a type of boiler that has found favour in some quarters, but decried in others. Developed many years ago by the designer whose name it bears, the Scott, unlike the simple design described before, has water tubes arranged across the centre line. In its original form it was used in conjunction with a flat flame. Figure 7.4 is a view with the end casing removed. Like all water tube boilers a casing lined with fireproof material, white asbestos, is needed to contain the heat. A later and more often used pattern is indicated in figure 7.5 and in this design 'U' tubes are fitted, equally spaced along the boiler drum, with firing being done by a torch type burner directed through the tunnel formed by the tubes and the bottom of the drum. Many found satisfaction with this simple layout in which circulation is aided by arranging that one end of each watertube is fitted higher in the drum than the other. Further improvement can be made by giving each water tube a complete loop, and figure 7.6 gives a picture of this scheme. This type of boiler is very suitable for narrow

63

Introducing Model Marine Steam

beamed boats and furthermore, if reduction in height is required then the boiler can be mounted on its side, figure 7.7a, at an angle, figure 7.7b, and if extra fast steam raising is required then the arrangement in figure 7.7c will allow the use of two burners of the torch type. A good design for a Scott boiler, plus additional information on high efficiency steam plants, is to be found in the book 'Experimental Flash Steam' by Rayman and Benson, published by Argus Books, though out of print.

FLASH STEAM

The term 'flash steam' is often bandied around, and the Scott is sometimes referred to as 'semi-flash'. Flash steam boilers are among the simplest designs in their basic forms. The principle used is as follows; a single tube is coiled around the furnace, water is pumped in one end and steam at high pressure comes out the other. More correctly known as mono-tube boilers, the flash boiler has generally been used for racing boats where extra high pressures are required, but as long as a good water feed is maintained it can be worked at lower pressures for other types of craft, and in this respect has been somewhat neglected. The Achilles heel of the design is, as mentioned, the need for a constant and reliable water feed which has caused so many racing boats to fail in the past, but this should be easier to solve for slower moving boats. Mono-tube boilers have in the past been used for commercial plants, and pressures generated can be very high, 2000 lbs/sq. in. and over being common; despite the high pressures they are probably one of the safest steam producers for the following reasons. If the tube fails then steam supply to the engine is cut off, pumps cease to work and as there is no great water capacity, the thing just shuts down.

For high pressure work stainless steel is the recommended material for mono-tube boilers and copper has been used successfully for those worked at the lower pressures generally used. The tube must be seamless, solid drawn, and soft for easy working. A tapered mandrel, figure 7.8, is used to form the coil. A length of approximately 20 feet of the tube is taken and one half is wound on the mandrel followed by the rest wound back over the first coils. When the coils are removed from the mandrel they are pulled apart so that hot gases can make their way through and around

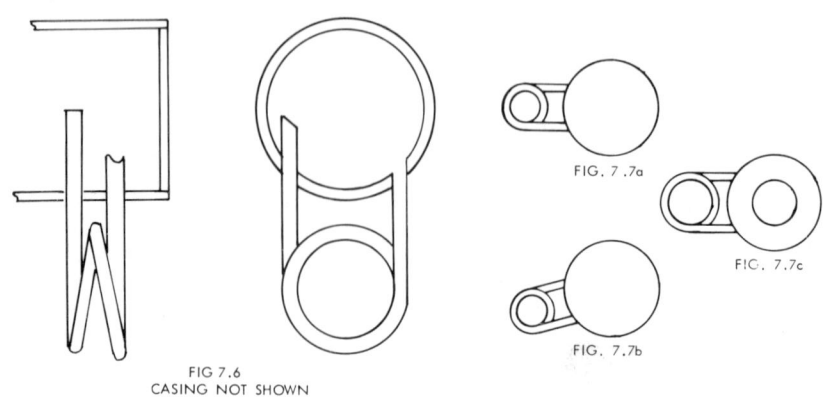

FIG 7.6
CASING NOT SHOWN

FIG. 7.7a

FIG. 7.7b

FIG. 7.7c

Watertube Boilers

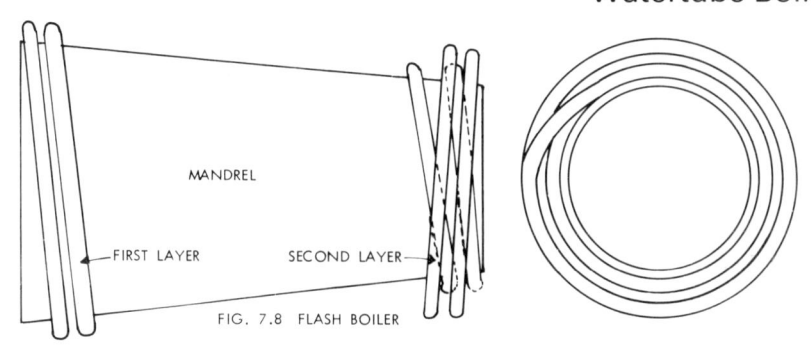

FIG. 7.8 FLASH BOILER

the coils, and the whole is encased similar to the Scott. Because the flash boiler has no real water capacity neither gauges to assess the water nor safety valves are fitted. It is essential however, to have efficient non-return valves on the pumps. Two pumps are required for a flash boiler, a hand pump in order to provide the initial water flow and an engine-driven one to maintain it.

While the flash boiler is generally used for model marine purposes in the horizontal form, there is no reason why it should not be used in a vertical form with the tube coils around the sides of the boiler casing. In this arrangement it would be possible to use solid fuels or burners with a less fierce flame than that generated by the traditional blowtorch. When used in this form for steam cars of yesteryear, the single tube was paralleled by others, in effect increasing the heating surface without increasing the length of tube through which the steam had to pass. Other arrangements of tubes in a flash boiler are possible, e.g. in a horizontal form two coils could be used in parallel for using with twin lamps or they could be arranged as a figure of eight shape, again using two lamps. In this field there is plenty of room for the experimenter to try out new ideas.

For the builder of steam launches, where vertical type boilers are common, it might be worth trying a type of boiler not often seen modelled but still used for full-size launch work in the U.S.A., and one that has the reputation of being an efficient producer of steam. This is the 'Lune Valley' type, and while the full-sized version uses steel tubing, our miniature could quite well be made of copper. In essentials there is a water/steam drum fitted with a series of helical coils of water tubes around its circumference; the assembly is housed in a drum type housing lined with a fireproof material and firing would be a flat circular lamp of the type more familiar to the domestic gas stove. With correct balancing of the air and gas or oil supplies, steam would be produced at a high rate, and like most watertube boilers, it could be worked at high pressures if required. Rather than use high pressures, some fast steam raisers could be used to reduce the amount of space taken up in a boat, so that the final layout, particularly in launches, bears a close relation to its full-size counterpart.

Water tube boilers are not so popular in model marine work as the firetube types, but they have one advantage over the firetube type in that leaks occurring after completion or that develop during service are more easily remedied as most joints are readily accessible.

Chapter Eight

Boiler Construction

Boiler construction causes the model marine engineer more headaches than most other items in a steam plant, for while he or she is prepared to learn the techniques of machining in order to build the engine, difficulty is found in the work needed to make the boiler. Most operations, apart from the actual jointing, can be performed with just the hand tools found in most home workshops, except for some simple machining to produce the bushes and fittings, and even these can be bought if so desired. The only technique that may have to be acquired is that of hard soldering, and it is this aspect of the work that daunts so many.

MATERIALS
In choosing materials, factors to be considered are:- ease of working, ease of jointing, safety in use and longevity of life. The commonest material used in model marine boilers and one that satisfies these requirements is copper; this is a metal that is very ductile when soft. It becomes hard when worked but can readily be returned to a soft state by heating to a bright red and plunging into cold water. Jointing by silver soldering, hard soldering (brazing) or welding with modern methods is comparatively easy; it has a good tensile strength, suffers little from corrosion, and is gifted with a long life — all of which make it by far the best choice for boilers constructed for model steamers.

Many mass-produced commercial boilers in the smaller sizes are made of brass and although many find satisfaction in the use of the resulting product, for the amateur's position the material is not such a good one to use as is copper, and cases have been reported where the metal has deteriorated over a long period of use. Brass is an alloy of zinc and copper and, like all alloys, its strength and capabilities will depend on the proportions of the component metals. The continual heating and cooling encountered in a boiler, and the fact that the brass usually obtained by the amateur constructor has an unknown composition, gives cause for the writers to consider brass a very second choice and in some cases a bad one at that.

With commercial boilers the position is slightly different, for the manufacturer will usually dictate the type of brass to be supplied. With the current use of copper for domestic plumbing there is little difficulty in getting supplies of our first choice and brass should be relegated to a secondary choice. Brass is often used for the pressure tanks of petrol and paraffin torches, and personal experience has found one such tank that had developed minute holes,

Boiler Construction

due no doubt to what a writer in a contemporary magazine calls 'de-zincification'. Whatever metal is used, make sure it comes from a reputable source, and in the case of brass boilers give them more care and retest more often than with copper equivalents.

Brass, like copper, can easily be jointed and in the same way. Also, like copper it will work-harden and it can be softened in a like fashion to the base material. When jointing brass use a lower melting point solder and keep the temperature down below that which you would use for copper; do not be tempted as others have in the past and use soft solder for making the joints. The apparent ease of soft soldering is a fallacy. It is as easy to hard solder and in any case the result is much more satisfactory.

The final choice generally open and one that is not to be recommended for small boilers is steel. While steel has a high tensile strength, the most obvious objection to its use is its liability to rusting, and in a marine environment the possibility of external rusting over that experienced by land-based equipment will of course add to the problem. Attempts have been made to plate the metal with a non-rusting medium without much success, and although large scale model locomotives make use of steel the required testing is more stringent and re-testing is more frequent. Very few model marine boilers have been constructed using this material

An immaculate example of a high speed straight running launch fitted with a flash steam boiler and Stuart Turner Sun engine.

67

Introducing Model Marine Steam

A historic boat on display, the late Mr. Johnson's Nippy (West London M.P.B.C.), as restored by Lt. Cdr. A. Greenhalgh R.N.Retd. Note the centre flue boiler with blowlamp inserted from aft and the forward position of the engine.

and then mainly for experimental work where the short life of the boiler was acceptable and where high pressures were to be used. Suitable stainless steels could be used but then sophisticated welding methods are usually required for jointing the metal, and the techniques and equipment are not to be found in the average amateur's workshop. On the other hand stainless steel tube, preferably solid drawn, is ideal for 'flash' boilers, and in the jointing, compression joints have been found satisfactory. One problem often encountered is that drawn tube tends to be hard and difficult to bend into the coils required for a flash boiler, therefore the constructor should try and get a malleable grade of tube for this work.

The three metals, copper, brass and steel, in that order, are generally accepted as the materials to use in boiler making, but others in the non-ferrous groups of metals or alloys have also been used on occasion, although in most cases the use of these other metals, mainly the bronzes, will be ruled out of court on the grounds of economic costs alone. Alloys such as phosphor-bronze are, however, to be recommended for making boiler fittings and bushes in preference to the more common brass. If at all possible eliminate the use of brass from anything that is to be permanently fixed to the boiler.

Strange as it may seem in view of its low melting point, aluminium has been used for low pressure boilers, where it could be arranged for the heat source to be shut down as soon as the water level became low or ran out. But unless serious experiments under strict safety controlled conditions are to be carried out, the use of this metal is not to be countenanced.

68

Boiler Construction

METHOD

Boiler construction methods have changed a lot in the years following World War II, for whereas before that time a lot of boilers were built with riveting and soft solder, and brazing was usually done using borax as a flux with brass spelter as the jointing medium, today the use of sophisticated fluxes and silver solders, made with the object of making flame brazing a more practical process, ensures that it is possible for anyone to make a satisfactory hard soldered joint, hence the quality of boiler work has improved considerably.

If the reader is confused by the terms hard soldering and brazing it must be said that the two terms are synonymous to all intents and purposes. In fact brazing generally refers to the use of a flame torch with a brass spelter while silver soldering uses an alloy solder and in fact from this point on, in the interests of uniformity, the term silver brazing, as used by Johnson Matthey, will only be used. Improved solders and fluxes have been accompanied by a better type of selection of brazing torches, although in the not so distant past many a boiler has been built using a petrol or paraffin blowlamp, in fact it is possible to use the blowlamp that will be used to fire the boiler to silver braze the said boiler together. Generally the amateur craftsman has gone over to the use of a self-blowing liquid gas type of blow torch using propane or butane gas supplied in replaceable cylinders. Both types are safe in use if basic safety precautions are taken. For the smaller jobs gas burners using the throwaway canister of liquid gas can be used and it is a useful practice if the model marine engineer includes such a torch in his kit, for it can be taken to the pondside ready for any emergency repairs.

With the increased availability of oxy-acetylene welding equipment some constructors use this to weld their boilers together, but for most the use of a flame torch is still the most popular choice and in such a basic book as this, it is not intended to go into the aspects of oxy-acetylene welding.

While jointing methods have changed, the pieces that go to make a complete boiler look very much the same as they always have, albeit with small modifications to take care of the new techniques. Boiler shells, barrels or drums (the terms vary from builder to builder) are best made out of solid drawn tube as this is the strongest form, but if no tube is available then the shell can be formed from plate rolled to shape and jointed. Figure 8.1 gives the idea using an overlap joint which is held together during silver brazing by several rivets. In the rivet and soft solder days the joint would have been made with the rivets as the holding factor and soft solder would have served as a caulking material. With silver brazing it is the solder that holds the joint and the rivets are only there to keep the pieces together during the jointing process.

A better method of making a joint in a rolled plate is shown in figure 8.2. The two edges of the plate are slit at regular intervals with a saw as shown, before rolling. The plate is rolled to shape and before the final closure is made the 'tabs' are bent alternately up and down, i.e. all the 'A's' are bent up and all the

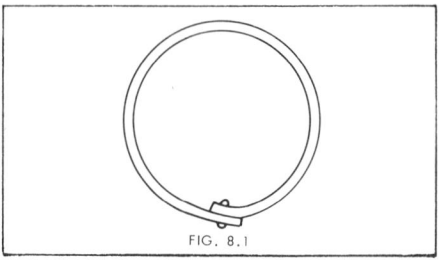

FIG. 8.1

Introducing Model Marine Steam

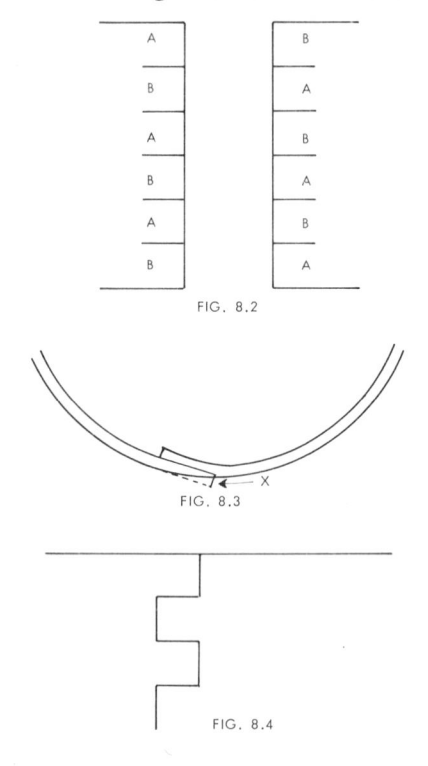

FIG. 8.2

FIG. 8.3

FIG. 8.4

'B's' down, so that when the final closure is made and the edges brought together an interlocking joint is formed — again a few rivets hold the work during soldering and the resulting joint seen end on will look like figure 8.3. To make a nice looking job from the outside the part marked 'X' can be filed off to conform with the curve of the rest of the shell. For the purpose in view it is not necessary for the inside to be cleaned up, although when this 'coppersmith's joint' is used for utensils the inside is always cleaned up. The resulting joint viewed from the outside will be seen as a bronze zig-zag on the face of the copper, figure 8.4.

End plates of boilers are formed from sheet materials, although on occasion castings have been used, but sheet is a better choice for one can be sure that no problems will arise from flaws in the material that are likely to be present in casting. To make the formed plate shown in section as figure 8.5, a former is required and this should be of as strong a material as available — steel or iron for preference, although a good hard wood will suffice if only one or two plates are to be formed. The former should be made of such a size that it will fit the final inside dimension of the plate, and since most of the boilers used in marine work are of cylindrical shape, the former can be turned easily on a lathe. Make it thicker than the depth of the plate's flange and ensure that one edge is well rounded; never have sharp changes in contour when forming plates. In fact, this is a good precept to follow in all metalwork.

Cut the plate from sheet of a diameter equal to the inside diameter of the shell plus twice the flange depth plus a small amount for working. Soften the sheet and mount the sheet plus the former in the vice, figure 8.6. Not shown here, but necessary, is protection between the jaw and the plate, unless your vice has smooth jaws. Commence at the top and beat the plate over the former in easy stages, turning both plate and former in the vice as you work round the perimeter. Figure 8.7 shows a plate partly formed. Don't let the metal get hard but repeat the softening process often. It is better to take time on this than risk having a plate fracture. When the plate is finally formed the outside edge can be trimmed by filing or by turning in the lathe. If the flange is too tight to go into the shell, it can be fitted by filing or taking a skim off in the lathe. Some model engineers deliberately make the formed plate bigger on the outside diameter in order that metal can be turned off in the lathe to provide a good mating surface with the inside of the

Boiler Construction

shell. Providing that not too much metal is removed from the plate this will prove a good way of ensuring close contact between the surface to be jointed, for as in all soldered surfaces, the better the matching of the joint the stronger the final result. Since the joint effectively unites the adjoining pieces into one entity, a small reduction in the thickness of the flange is acceptable.

The use of this type of former is not restricted to circular plates and if it is necessary to make plates of other shapes, the same principle can be used. Of course the plate will have to be made by some method other than by turning and generally the use of a hacksaw and file is called for, except for those lucky enough to have milling or shaping machines. Gentle work with the hammer plus close attention to the hardening of the metal are the clues to success in forming metal plates; get practice in by making the simple circular ones before you go onto the more exotic shapes required for loco type boilers, petrol tanks or the like.

The fitting of tubes into plates would seem to be an easy task, but some people have difficulty and this usually comes about because insufficient care is taken in the drilling of the required holes. Follow the precept that a drilled hole is rarely a circular one and drill all holes for tubes undersize and reamer to the required size. Tubes should be a good fit in their holes so that they do not move about during the jointing process and it is a good practice to make a minute countersink on the outside edge of the hole in the plate as in figure 8.8, then expand the tube by gentle pressure from a ball pein hammer rotated against the tube end. Various means of fixing tubes, apart from soldering, have been tried in the past. One such made use of an expanding former which was inserted in the tube, expanded and rotated so that the tube had a ring formed as in figure 8.9, hardly a practical

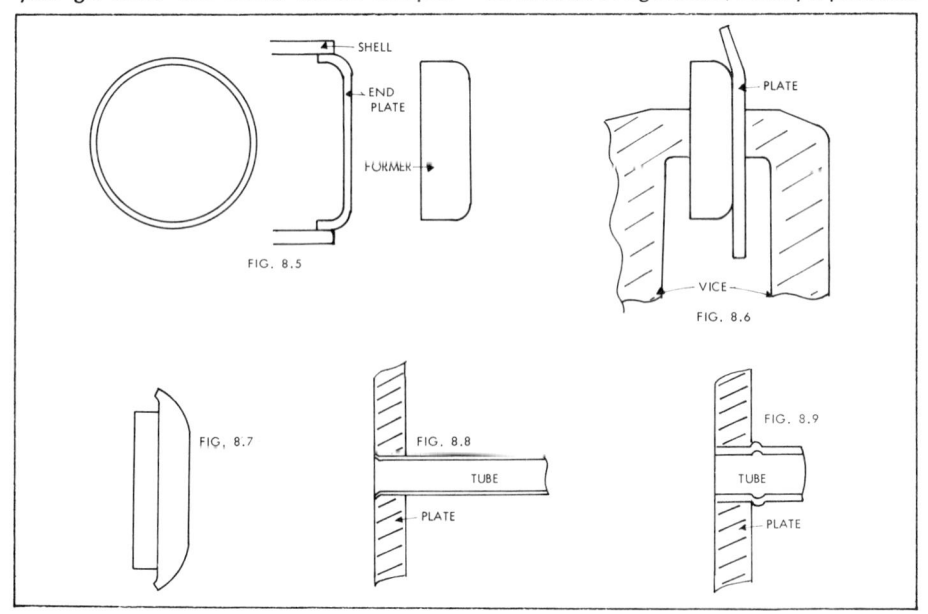

FIG. 8.5

FIG. 8.6

FIG. 8.7

FIG. 8.8

FIG. 8.9

71

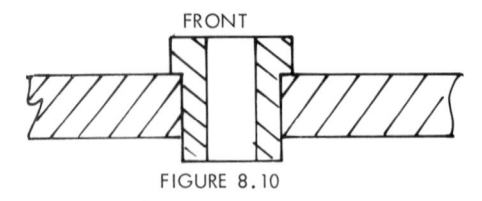

Introducing Model Marine Steam

FIGURE 8.10

method for the very small boiler but one that proved satisfactory in large units, having the virtue of not requiring welding.

The same principle of expansion to hold a part in place can be applied to the bushes, figure 8.10. These should also be a good fit in the hole and after insertion, the front of the bush should be laid on a hard surface and the rear hit with a hammer to burr the outside edge over slightly. This will hold the piece in place during subsequent operations. Remember though to run a tap through the bush after doing this to ensure that the thread is clean before the boiler is finished.

SILVER BRAZING

Earlier, the term silver brazing was introduced. This is the term used by Johnson Matthey and in case the reader is unaware of that firm, a short explanation will be helpful. Johnson Matthey Metals Ltd. are a major supplier of solders and fluxes for the hard jointing of metals and they have paid particular attention to the needs of the amateur or small-time professional so that their name is synonymous with the process of silver brazing with a flame torch. Their Easy-Flo fluxes and solders are to be recommended for our purposes.

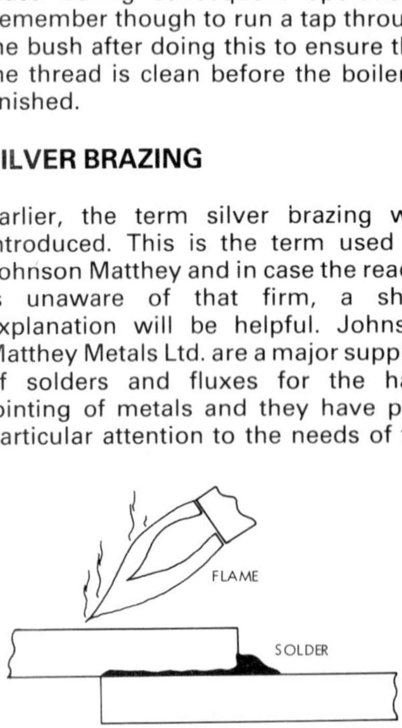

Since we are dealing with materials that contain both cadmium and zinc, attention to the safety precautions contained in the Johnson Matthey Leaflet 1100:105 are worth studying, and readers are advised to obtain a copy from the company.

Silver brazing, low temperature brazing, silver soldering and hard soldering are all terms used for basically the same process, i.e. brazing in the temperature range 600°C to 850°C using filler alloys based mainly on the metals silver and copper but also containing either cadmium or zinc or sometimes both. The fluxes used contain alkali metal fluoborates which can cause skin irritation and particular attention should be paid to personal cleanliness – any cuts should be covered at once.

The most essential thing about silver brazing is to have both pieces that are to be jointed perfectly clean before commencing the heating process. After cleaning, with a file, wet and dry paper or wire wool, apply a light coating of flux before assembly and hold the pieces together, with rivets if possible or otherwise clamps, while giving sufficient heat to make the joint. When the flux takes on a glass-like appearance, the solder can be applied. This judgement will come with practice and it is as well to try out some test pieces before setting about the main business.

The solder will run by capillary action toward the point of greatest heat, something that is worth remembering, for by heating in the right place solder can be directed to unseen parts, figure 8.11. In making most small boilers the operation can usually be performed in

FIGURE 8.11

Boiler Construction

two or three stages and once the work is prepared can be carried out in a short space of time. For instance, when making the common centre flue boiler, the cross tubes would be fitted and brazed into the centre flue using Easy-Flo solder which has a melting point of 620°C to 630°C, and after cooling and cleaning the whole of the boiler would be assembled and then brazed with Easy-Flo No.2 which has a lower melting point of 608°C to 617°C. This scheme of using the solder with the highest melting point for initial operations does help to ensure that the risk of undoing previous work is reduced to a minimum, although many find it easy enough to use the one grade solder throughout. This is possible because remelting temperatures are higher than the original soldering temperature.

One of the difficulties encountered by the beginner is caused by the fact that copper is a very good conductor of heat, a property that makes it good for use in a boiler but which can cause occasional problems when brazing pieces together. In order to overcome any possible problems, heat should be conserved by surrounding the workpiece with firebricks. For small work a hearth as marketed by Kenneth Johns, figure 8.12, can be recommended. After completion of the brazing operation the work should be allowed to cool down somewhat and then, while still warm, immersed in a weak solution of sulphuric acid and water to clean off the remaining flux. For those who have objections to keeping such a solution on hand the work can be dipped into water and the flux removed using a wire brush; however, the resulting appearance by using this method is not as good as the acid bath system.

Fig. 8·12 A brazing hearth conserves heat during brazing operations.

BOILER FITTINGS

Usually the simple boiler is only fitted with a plug for filling and a safety valve, the latter being the most essential fitting of all and one which must be maintained in a good condition. While this may suit a boiler that has the fuel capacity geared to run out at the same time that the water is exhausted, when it is required to have longer runs and to steam larger engines, then some additional fittings are required to assist in the running. All fittings should be arranged to screw into

Introducing Model Marine Steam

FIGURE 8.13

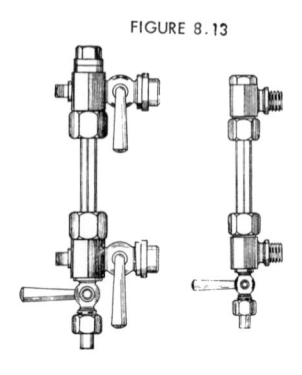

the boiler by the use of bushes, figure 8.10. The interior screw thread should be a suitable size for each fitting. One of the first essentials is to know what the water content of the boiler is at any time and this is obtained by the provision of a water gauge, figure 8.13. Water gauges should always have a blow-down cock in order to clear any bubbles that may be present in the gauge glass, also three-cock gauges are useful in case of a gauge glass breaking because the additional two cocks can shut off entry of steam and water to the gauge. Glass breakage can be reduced if the glands holding the packing, usually a piece of rubber tube or an 'O' ring, are not over-tightened. Finger tight is in most cases sufficient.

A pump of some sort is fitted to feed water into the boiler while it is running. In order that water can be pumped in, the provision of one or more non-return valves is required. Figure 8.14 shows a section through such a valve and it will be seen that water pumped in will lift the ball but on cessation of pumping the ball will seal the feed line against leakage from the boiler. A check on the boiler pressure is needed where increased pressures used for more sophisticated plants are in use and this is done by fitting of a pressure gauge. This is one fitting which is beyond the scope of most amateurs to construct and it is necessary that the best one available should be used. Go to a reliable supplier for this and fit the biggest one within reason that can be accommodated in the boat.

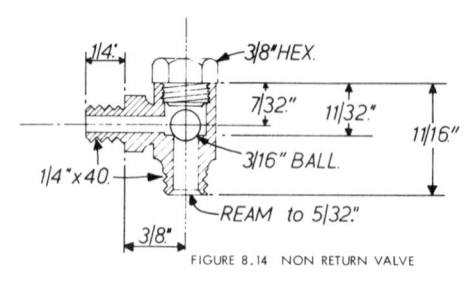

These four items, Safety Valve, Water Gauge, Non-return Valve (clack) and Pressure Gauge are all familiar items on most boats that are operated in a serious manner, and which make use of boiler pressures higher than those employed in the simpler forms of steam plant. Additional valves may be fitted to supply other items that the constructors feel necessary, e.g. whistles. In the case of solid fuel boilers, a valve to control a blower in the smoke box will be needed. However, for all boilers it can be said that the four fittings listed above are the ones essential to operations. Fittings may be bought from the many suppliers of model goods but for those modellers who desire to make their own, M.A.P Plan LO42, although primarily geared to the interest of the live steam locomotive, will be of use.

TESTING

The last part of this chapter is the most important, for with the growing interest in steam there is always the concern that because of poor workmanship, a bad accident due to boiler failure will occur. In the interest of the precept that should be followed by all live steamers, that it is

FIGURE 8.14 NON RETURN VALVE

Boiler Construction

'Safety First and Always', the proper testing and maintenance of all pressure vessels is essential. We use the term pressure vessels because in addition to boilers the same danger from explosion applies to blowlamp containers and the like. Any pressure vessel that is faulty is a potential bomb and consequences could be serious; fortunately serious accidents from such a failure are non-existent at the present time, but only because most builders take care in construction and make sure by testing their work.

To test a pressure vessel of the sort that will be used by marine modellers is basically a simple operation and uses the principle that for all practical purposes water is incompressible. If this method is used for testing a boiler or the like to destruction it can be done without danger to life or limb. First remove all the fittings except the non-return valve, which should be connected to a hand pump. Plug all the bushes except the safety valve hole and then *completely* fill the boiler with water, and we mean completely. Great care should be taken to ensure that no air pockets are left and in most cases, unless the boiler is of unusual construction, filling with water by pumping until it comes out of the safety valve hole will ensure this. Using an adaptor, connect a master pressure gauge to the safety valve hole; this master gauge should be one that is kept for the purpose and is known to be accurate. Most model engineering societies have access to one and will be pleased to assist in the operation.

The boiler is now full of water and small movements of the pump will immediately send up the pressure. This should be increased until the pressure is twice the designed working pressure. Hold the pressure and examine the boiler for any leaks which will be indicated by weeps of water. Mark any found, empty the boiler and make good by brazing, then re-test as before. It should only be necessary to hold the pressure for the time it takes to make a thorough examination. Some authorities specify a release of pressure and restoration to test pressure several times, but if the pressure is held the first time this indicated that things are satisfactory and there seems little point in repeating the process.

Restore all the fittings and test that the safety valve will release the pressure at the correct point and also that it will let off steam as fast as the boiler can make it.

Re-testing of the boiler should take place at least every second year to one-an-a-half times the working pressure, but since there is little trouble in setting up the test many will test each year. When re-testing check the condition of the fittings, renew the safety valve spring, the clack ball, and the gauge glass; if in doubt, check the pressure gauge against a master gauge.

Chapter Nine

Firing and Fuels

The design of a boiler is governed by a number of factors, not the least of which is how it is to be fired and what fuel is to be used. As far as fuels are concerned there are three options open, liquid fuel, liquefied gas and solid fuels.

Liquid fuels include methylated spirits (alcohol), petrol (gasolene), paraffin (kerosene) and fuel oil. Burners and furnaces are varied and some types will suit only one kind of fuel while others will cater for one or more, albeit with minor modifications.

It is necessary for the builder to know the characteristics, advantages and disadvantages of possible fuels so that his or her choice shall serve the purpose best, and the following short résumé of the common fuels is intended to give some guidance on the subject. It is not intended to be a complete exposé, but should help in the making of a decision as to what fuel to use.

Methylated Spirits, known also as wood alcohol in some places, has been for many years the basic fuel in the many simple units offered commercially and to a lesser degree in the more sophisticated ones. It burns well with an intense flame but is liable to give off unpleasant fumes, which have earned it the name in the past of a 'poison gas plant', and in use it is essential to give the flame plenty of ventilation. It is easily obtainable on the domestic market but suffers from the safety angle inasmuch that spilt spirit will spread rapidly across any surface and readily ignite. In strong light conditions, such as bright sunlight, the flame is practically invisible and is thus a safety hazard. Its use in the model world is being superseded by solidified alcohol tablets such as Meta, Mamod etc.

Naphtha has been used on occasion by a few people in this country and one form is the solid derivative sold as the common fire lighter. The heat from these tablets is not as great as from those sold for camping purposes and they tend to burn with a lot of smoke. It is interesting to note that in the U.S.A., full size launches were made at one time that boiled naptha in the boiler and used the vapour as steam in the engine, passing the exhaust to the burner to fire the boiler. It was an ingenious scheme to overcome some aspects of their boiler regulations but as far as is known the idea was never tried in a model.

Paraffin is one of the more commonly used fuels favoured by the amateur constructor, and it gives plenty of heat when burnt in the primus type of blowtorch. The liquid itself is liable to make an oily mess in a boat if spilt and an added disadvantage is that burners are liable to flood or blow out while running, the ensuing conflagration being

Firing & Fuels

spectacular and usually damaging. If the lamp goes out, the liquid deposited will take some time to clear from the boat as the evaporation rate is low and it is not recommended that the lamp be re-lighted until all paraffin is clear of the interior. This last is not such a problem for users of petrol, which evaporates quicker and furthermore does not attract dirt in the same way that paraffin appears to. It is suggested that the leadless grades of petrol to be obtained if possible, in preference to road spirit; the latter is commonly used in spite of the lead additive but in the interest of safety, leaded fuel should only be used out of doors and the user should avoid inhaling the fumes. Petrol is a cleanly burning fuel.

Liquid gas, usually Propane or Butane, has been increasing in popularity in recent years and is generally used in the throw-away canisters sold for camping enthusiasts. Gas has a lot to commend it as an energy medium, and the easy lighting of the burners plus the cleanliness of burning and general convenience makes it the fuel of the future.

Users of liquefied gases should bear in mind the need to provide plenty of ventilation and also that most of these gases are heavier than air, so that if the burner does go out and the hull becomes full of gas, it is necessary to clear it by turning the hull upside down for a short while. This procedure obviously means that all the pieces inside the boat need a secure fixing in case of trouble. Of course in the event of a major conflagration one can follow the example of so many in the past and use the lake as an extinguisher by dunking the boat below the surface. However,

Getting a blowlamp started. Jack Humpish from Heaton is aided by wife Gladys at a straight running regatta at St. Albans.

Introducing Model Marine Steam

careful handling will eliminate the need for such drastic action if simple and commonsense precautions are taken during operation. Safety first and always.

As well as throw-away camping containers, it is possible to use the larger re-chargeable cylinders, and users of both these kinds of container need have no fear about safety as the suppliers are bound by law to ensure that regular safety checks are carried out. If the builder decides to make his own container, an exercise that is frowned upon by the authorities, then he should make sure that in use he leaves sufficient space in the container for gas to fill; two thirds full of liquid is a safe figure.

On the subject of containers for fuel, when they are to be used under pressure they should be tested in the same way and at the same frequency as the boiler. Any signs of failure or leakage that cannot be repaired with 100% satisfaction should be the reason for discarding the container and replacing it. Likewise, in the case of throwaway liquid gas containers, if damage to the container is sustained, replace it — the cost of a new one is worth the feeling of additional safety.

In contrast to the cleanliness of canned gas, solid fuels, (and in this context is meant of course the older fuels such as wood and coal and not the modern solid alcohol derivatives) are generally dirty in use, and after a day's running most such boats become very soiled, requiring a lot of cleaning. It is also quite likely that the operator will become as dirty as the boat! The small band of devotees of solid fuel generally use Welsh steam coal, not so easy to obtain today as of yore, and seem to enjoy the fun of stoking up. The disadvantage of looking like a coal miner after a day's boating is ranked as part of the fun! Wood is rarely used except for the prime purpose of initial steam raising.

BURNERS

The choice of a burner for a marine boiler is very much one of individual preference whatever fuel is to be used. For the purchaser of one commercial plant it will be Hobson's Choice if the equipment is to be used as supplied by the manufacturer. For the simpler plants using methylated spirits, quite often a simple burner of the type shown in figure 9.1 is used. In essentials it consists of an open top tank filled with a fireproof absorbent material, having the open side closed by a piece of wire gauze. Care should be taken when using this type of burner that it is not overfilled, causing spirit to run over before and after lighting. It sometimes happens that the heat will cause spirit to bubble over and catch fire outside the tank. A variation of this burner is one where a separate tank is used for storage and the burner consists of a tube extension with the end closed and a part of the top open, filled again with fire-resistant material. In section, the arrangement is like that in figure 9.2. A further variant using wicks can be made as in figure 9.3, this being a type that found favour for small water tube boilers, and which is probably more economic in the use of spirit while still providing all the heat required.

Simple burners of the type described all show tendencies to flood due to the uncontrolled supply of spirit. One way of controlling the flow is to use two tanks and a 'chicken hopper feed' arrangement as in figure 9.4. The principle is simple and supply to the auxiliary tank only occurs when the lower part of the supply pipe from the main tank is uncovered, so allowing air into the tank. It is called a 'chicken hopper feed' because,

Firing & Fuels

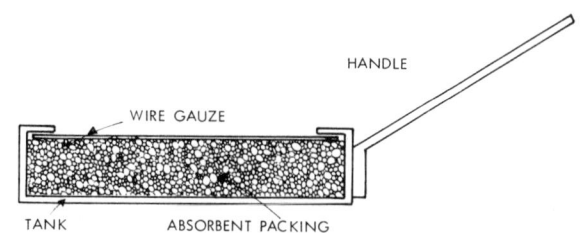

FIGURE 9.1 ALCOHOL BURNER (SECTIONED)

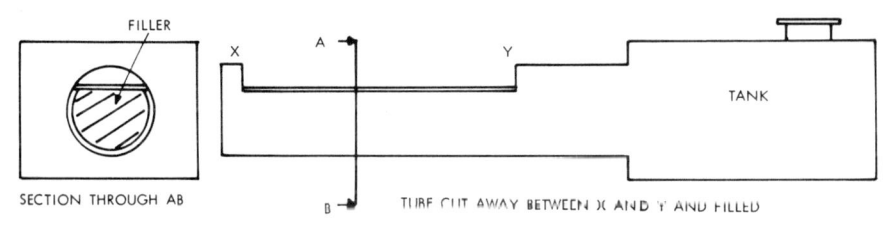

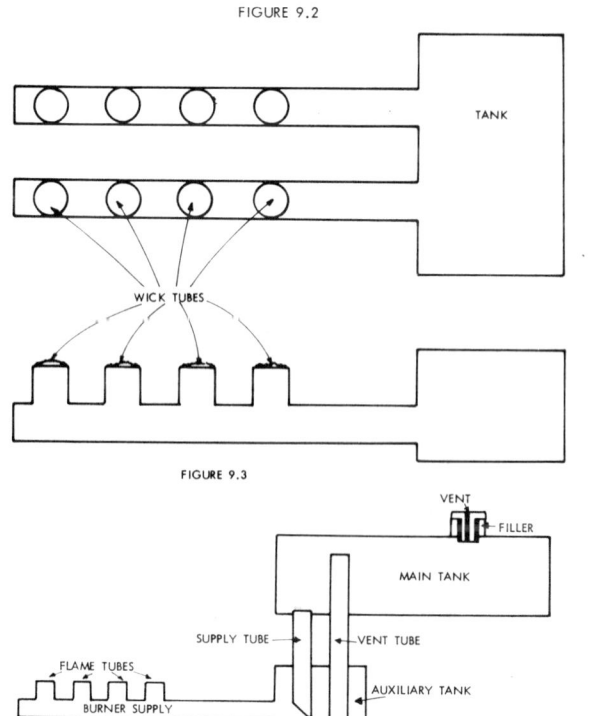

FIGURE 9.2

FIGURE 9.3

FIGURE 9.4

79

Introducing Model Marine Steam

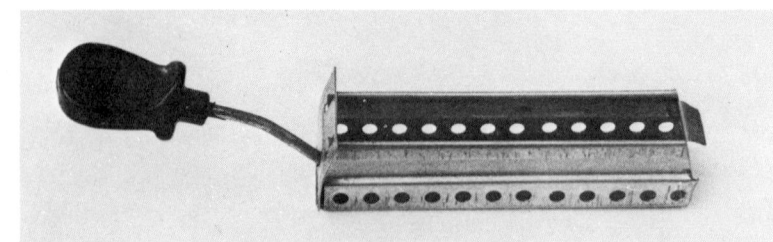

Fig. 9·5

Below Fig. 9·6

as will easily be recognised, this is the system used in a more primitive form by the bird fancier for maintaining the drinking water supply in his aviaries.

Conversion of a spirit-fired boiler to one using solid alcohol fuel is easily achieved as the tank can be denuded of its filling and gauze, and the tablets then burnt in the resulting tray. Better still, a tray can easily be constructed as in figure 9.5, and it should be noted that in order to allow the tablets to burn properly the sides of the tray should be perforated to allow air to pass through. All the burners mentioned are best suited to a water tube boiler, or even a simple pot boiler where the fire is located below the barrel. In building the burner, ensure that air is flowing through when in operation by leaving one end open and by making some air holes in the side of the casing. These can be fitted with sliding shutters to allow control of the air and the idea is used successfully in the boiler supplied to USE engines, designed for multi-cylinder engine use.

Commercially, the ST engine outfit uses the methylated spirit tank while Wilesco, Mamod and USE now use solid fuels, as pictures show. A development of the tray holder for this purpose is seen in one of the USE boilers where the tray is fixed and the boiler is hinged to allow easy re-charging of the fuel.

All liquid fuels have to be vaporized before they can be burnt with effect in our furnaces, and while methylated spirit will readily vaporize and burn without assistance in simple burners, this and other fuels when burnt in a more sophisticated plant have to be assisted to vaporize by preheating the supply. Generally methylated spirit is resticted to the simpler plants as cost usually precludes quantity usage, but if needed, burners of the Bunsen type are used with a secondary burner to heat the main supply. Figure 9.6 shows such a burner that was described in Model Boats magazine. Commercially the best known example of these burners were those used in the Japanese made Saito engines. The Saito was a little different from the Model Boats example in that the added heat was obtained by an extension of the fuel tank welded to the burner tube, as the photograph shows.

The principle of the Bunsen burner, figure 9.7, is employed in most lamps used for model work. Gas is passed under pressure through a fine nozzle

Firing & Fuels

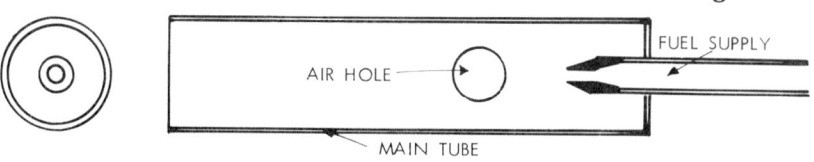

FIGURE 9.7   SIMPLE BUNSEN BURNER

and past an air intake into a mixing tube, where the gas and air mix to form a readily combustible combination. Burning occurs at the end of the tube. In the case of liquid gas the plain Bunsen burner can be used, as the gas will vaporize as soon as it is released from the container, so that in most cases no heating is required. However, on occasions when the rate of use of the gas is high, a refrigeration effect is generated in the container which slows gas delivery rate, and some heating has to be applied, usually by winding a steam pipe around the outside. (Caution – do not apply violent heat). This is not a common occurrence and will not trouble the average user.

For petrol or paraffin a burner of the type shown in figure 9.8 will prove satisfactory where it can be seen that the fuel is given some heat by the tube wound around the burner nozzle. The Bunsen principle is applied by directing the jet of vapour through the centre of the nozzle tube. Still obtainable are the one-time-common Primus nipples and their use is recommended. Problems usually arise because of the tendency of this type of burner to become blocked. The hole in the nipple is a minute one and a temporary remedy is to use a fine 'pricker' to unbung the hole. It is better though, to take the nipple out and give it a good clean, also blowing air through the supply tube to get rid of any more pieces of dirt that might be there. One solution to the problem of obtaining Primus nipples if they are in short supply is to use a valve-cum-nipple, as in figure 9.9. This type of nipple also has the advantages that fine regulation of the fuel supply is possible and clearance of dirt is made easier. With these types of burners the fuel is usually passed to the jet under pressure, this pressure being supplied by pumping up the container with air either from a built-in pump or by the use of a Schräder valve (as used on car tyres). When such a container is made, it is necessary to pressure test it with cold water in the same way as a boiler. It is also a good idea to fit a pressure gauge to the container so that a control is kept on the pressure. Many commercial blowlamps are fitted with a safety valve and again this is something that can be recommended, but arrange that the released gas or liquid is guided overboard and not confined between decks where it will provide a safety hazard.

The vaporizing type of blowlamp is not the only means of burning liquid fuel and there are several other ways that can be used. A common method with large furnaces is to use an atomizing burner. This is a method where the fuel is vaporized and mixed with air

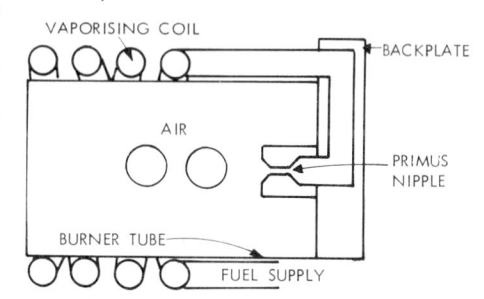

NOTE. IT IS SOMETIMES RECOMMENDED THAT VAPORISING COIL BE INSIDE TUBE FOR PARAFFIN

FIGURE 9.8

Introducing Model Marine Steam

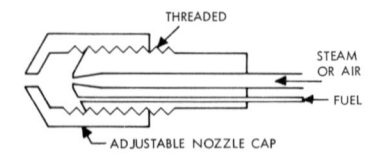

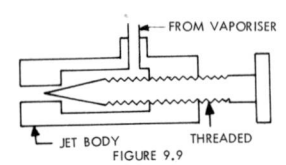

```
         THREADED
      /\/\/\/\——→  STEAM
  ———————————         OR AIR
  ————————————←—    FUEL
      \/\/\/\/
      ADJUSTABLE NOZZLE CAP
```

```
              FROM VAPORISER
         ———————↓
        /\/\/\/\
  ——————————————
  ——————————————
        \/\/\/\/
      JET BODY   ↑
                THREADED
          FIGURE 9.9
```

simultaneously as in figure 2.6. While not often used in model practice, this type of burner is particularly useful when a large quantity of heat is required, as in a racing boat using flash steam, and in such circumstances both the air and fuel supplied are pumped to the nozzle while running. The burner has the added advantage that if the engine should fail, because of a water supply failure, which is a problem that often besets a flash steam hydroplane, then pumping of fuel ceases and the burner goes out – a useful safety arrangement. Steam can be used instead of air, and in this case the practice is to have the fuel fed by a gentler means such as gravity, with the force of the steam jet causing a small vacuum effect to pull the fuel into combination. Only a minute amount of steam is needed and air is burnt from the surrounding space in the furnace, plus of course the fact that high superheat steam, which should be used, is oxygen-rich and will in itself aid combustion. It might be worthwhile in the future, with diminishing oil supplies, to experiment with this type of burner to use up waste lubricating oil that would otherwise be discarded.

Pre-heating of the lamp is necessary when it is of the blowtorch variety and usually this is done by having a shallow tin with some rag soaked in methylated spirit or paraffin placed under the nozzle and ignited. The container is pumped up and when the lamp is hot the fuel is gradually turned on. As the vaporized fuel fires it will generate enough heat to keep running on its own, and the starting flame is withdrawn and extinguished. This procedure can be hastened, and made safer as well, if a metal screen is placed around the lamp. The safety aspect cannot be stressed too highly as, if the lamp is not properly heated when the fuel is turned on, the fuel will shoot out as a liquid and ignite in a long sheet of flame. Without a screen it can cause burns to anyone in its path. Be extra careful if using blowlamps in public places, especially when children are about, for the last thing that should happen is an accident to the onlookers. Safety always above everything else!

Liquid gas burners in general use are adapted from the burners used for D.I.Y. work. The procedure is to detach the burner from the can fitting and add an additional pipe between the two to suit the boat. These adaptations work very well but it must be kept in mind that the container should be used, if at all possible, in an upright or nearly upright position. When used horizontally there is insufficient gas space above the liquid, hence the supply tube is full of liquid and not the released gas that is wanted for combustion. Recently, specialized burners have been placed on the market for model marine use and the photograph shows a comparison between one of the new burners and a common gas burner. This type of fuel is one that will become more popular as time goes on and although the possible world oil shortage may not affect model marine very much, it is always a nice thought to know that the gas contained in the tank is not dependent on oil.

Chapter Ten

Auxiliaries

Once the basic units of a marine steam plant have been determined, the constructor will give some thought to additional items that will assist easy running or add to the general interest of a steamer. A simple outfit consisting of a boiler that contains just sufficient water for a short voyage will soon lose interest if steps are not taken to improve length of performance without the bother of cooling the boiler down and pouring water into a filler plug. An easy first step is to fit a hand pump so that the water can be topped up as required without stopping the engine. Hand pumping is advantageous even when more sophisticated forms of pumping are used, for the hand pump of the type shown in figure 10.1 will (a) always fill the boiler at the commencement of the run, and (b) if by chance water goes low then a few quick strokes of the hand lever will restore the level to a working one.

The hand pump, and indeed for that matter most water pumps, used in marine work make use of a piston moving to and fro in a cylinder, drawing in water from the supply on one stroke and delivering it under pressure to the boiler on the return. Water direction is achieved by the two non-return valves in the valve box shown on the left hand end of the cylinder in the figure. Several points need to be borne in mind when choosing or making a water pump:- that it should be big enough for the job is a fact that should not need to be stated, as it seems so obvious, but so often pumps fitted are nowhere near big enough. It is better to err on the large size as surplus pumped water can always be diverted overboard. With hand pumps, the only restrictions that will affect size are weight and available space, and of course the strength of the engineer's muscles. Weight need not be too much of a problem for in many cases it will only mean that less otherwise useless ballast will have to be carried.

Pump valves have to be watertight on their seating and care should be taken to ensure that the seating is flat and square with the waterway. This latter should be drilled undersize and reamed, on the principle that most drilled holes are not completely round. The valve face should be finished at the same setting as the reamered hole. The opposite outlet to the seating has to be such that water is not restricted and the problem here is to prevent the ball from actually seating on the outflow face. It is natural perversity that when a seating is required, a drilled hole will not serve the purpose; however, when not required a similar hole will effect a seal, of course. One way

83

Introducing Model Marine Steam

Fig. 10.1 An example of a commercially available hand pump, from Fyne Fort Fittings.

to ensure flow is to chisel several notches on the edge of the hole or to fit a screw that will check the travel of the ball. It can be noted that it is possible to make a pump with two separate non-return valves, so using commercial components, figure 10.2.

A design point to bear in mind with all water pumps is the need to avoid 'air locks' due to air trapped and compressing under pressure. Many pump failures can be attributed to this factor, and this is something from which the arrangement in figure 10.2 is likely to suffer. Air locks can nearly always be eliminated by the provision of a spigot on the end of the ram as in figure 10.3; the spigot entering the valve chamber reduces the amount of air trapped. Perhaps an even better arrangement is to have the ram itself enter the valve box. If valve boxes are situated below the waterline, or in the case of separate feed water tanks below the water level, normal filling of the boiler before steaming will eliminate most trapped air. Always arrange that in addition to the valves on the pump there is a non-return valve (clack) on the boiler. Many hand pumps have been made without a gland on the ram and while these may be satisfactory for a while when used submerged in a water tank, for general marine use they should be avoided and glands should always be fitted and maintained in a leakproof condition.

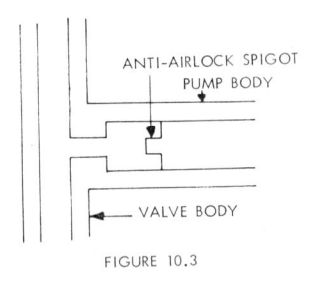

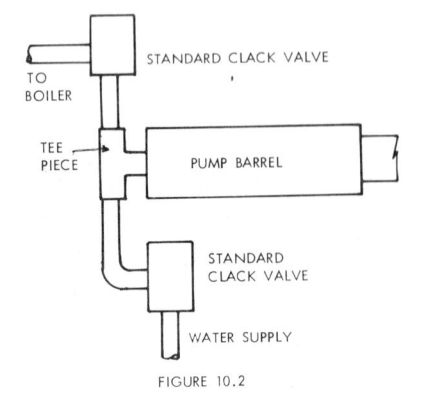

Having stressed the need for a leakproof gland, it is worthwhile indicating that the design of the hand levers of the pump will be beneficial if they can be arranged to avoid undue side pressure on the ram. The arrangement in figure 10.4 is one that is satisfactory in use; in a few

FIGURE 10.2

FIGURE 10.3

Auxiliaries

cases a tail to the ram or even a double ram in figure 10.5 will improve matters. In addition, the latter arrangement will enable water to be put into the boiler easier and faster than with a single ram.

While hand pumping will replace water in the boiler without the necessity to extinguish the fire, constant attention to the water level is still required and frequent visits to the pond side by the boat are called for in order to make the necessary checks on the water. Obviously, if a pump can be driven from the engine and the water supply matched to the rate of usage, then this chore can be eliminated. Engine-driven pumps are smaller both in stroke and bore than the hand pump, and are run at reduced speed from the engine by means of either spur gears or a worm and wheel arrangement. With the normal speed of a marine engine, some difficulty is likely to be experienced with maintaining a good seal on the valve faces due to ball bounce, and of course at engine speed the amount of water that has to be pumped would be small and the pump similarly very small; obviously it is better and easier to build a bigger pump and run it at slower than engine speed.

FIGURE 10.4

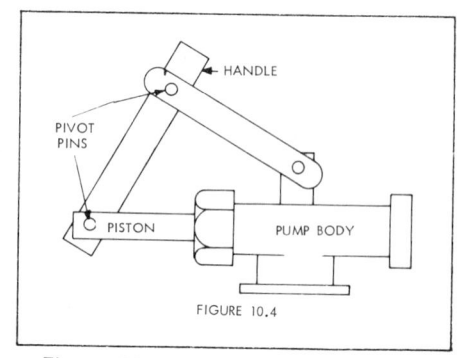

Figure 10.6 shows an arrangement for using a worm and wheel drive to the pump and in this case the pump is arranged parallel to the main shaft; also to drive the pump an eccentric on the secondary shaft is used. This arrangement is particularly good as (a) it reduces the overall width of the power unit and the gearing and (b) the eccentric drive makes for smooth and of course silent running with minimum friction losses. A worm drive like this can be easily lined up, although particular care should be taken to avoid the worm 'bottoming' on the wheel. When a spur drive is used, often the gear train is noisy, especially if insufficient care is taken in making the gear box frame which houses the gears.

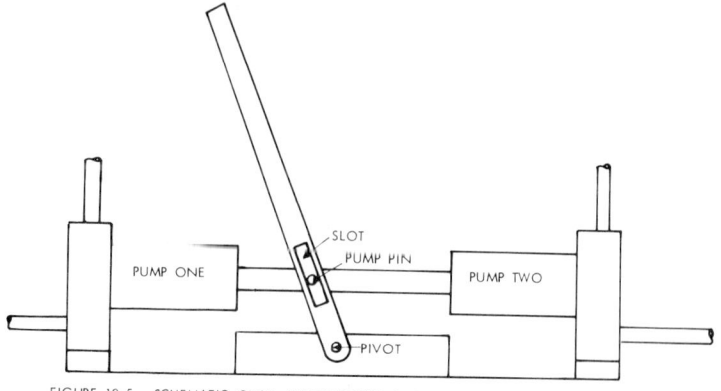

FIGURE 10.5 SCHEMATIC ONLY. VALVE BOXES AND HANDLE CAN BE FITTED WITH LINKS AS PER SINGLE RAM PUMP.

Introducing Model Marine Steam

Fig. 10·6 A worm drive (forward of engine) for a feed water pump.

Figure 10.7 shows a spur wheel drive and this type is most popular as spur gears are easily obtained from a number of sources; in the past, gears from old clocks have often been used. These gears are not really to be recommended as they are usually not man enough for the job. A crank-shaft drive of conventional pattern is shown which is mounted across the engine frame. Another means of driving the pump is by the use of a 'Scotch Crank' as in figure 10.8. With both a common or 'Scotch Crank', some means of adjusting the flow of water can be provided by arranging that the crank pin is movable to alternative positions on the crank disc. This method is often used but a better way of controlling water flow is by the use of a bypass valve which is just a screw-down valve fitted to a pipe in the supply line as in figure 10.9. Under running conditions, this valve is left open so that excess water is discharged overboard. The degree of opening required will be found by careful experiment and once found will not require much variation during normal running. Over the years this ar-

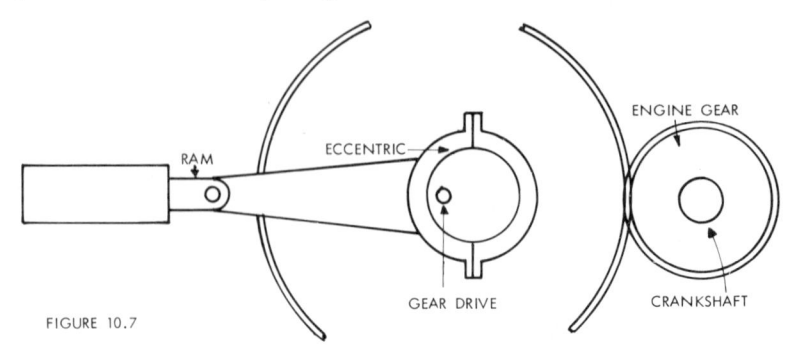

FIGURE 10.7

86

Auxiliaries

rangement has proved to be the easiest and most satisfactory way to control water supply from pumps.

Another method of water supply to boilers is to use an injector, but there are some major objections which effectively put it out of court for most model marine purposes. Injectors require a supply of *clean* water, as any impurities will effectively block the supply, and steam pressure is often critical; by and large the injector has to be worked under constant supervision, making it, like the hand pump, dependent on frequent docking for operation. However, for the man who likes to make everything himself, there is a challenge in making an injector – a task that beats so many good craftsmen.

For those who find an interest in the device, figure 10.10 gives a basic cross section of an injector. Water is fed via the inlet into a mixing chamber, steam is admitted via the first nozzle and shoots across the water supply into the combining cone, giving impetus to the water, and at the same time combining with it. The combined mass and speed of the now hot water (steam plus water) overcomes the resistance of the non-return valve and enters the boiler. Injectors use quite a lot of steam but much of the heat involved is put back into the boiler. Steam pressure is likely to be critical and most injectors will only work between narrow limits of boiler pressure. The water supply is also sometimes critical and adjustments of

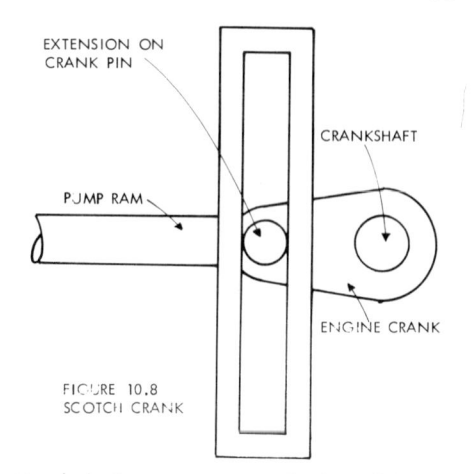

FIGURE 10.8 SCOTCH CRANK

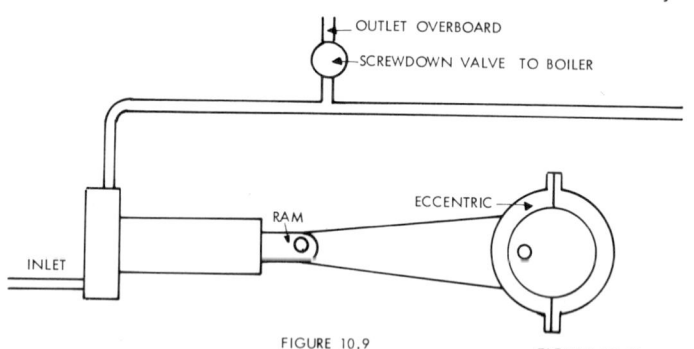

FIGURE 10.9

FIGURE 10.10

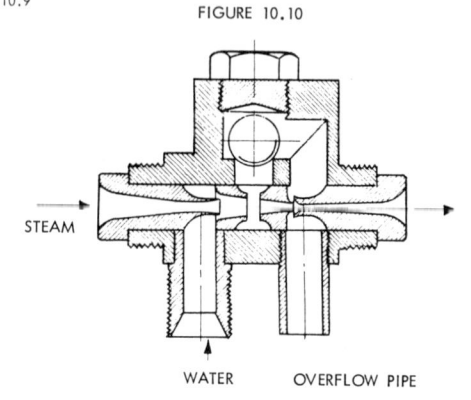

87

Introducing Model Marine Steam

both steam and water supply are needed during an injector's operation.

Whatever type of boiler feed is used, it should be the aim of the designer/builder to maintain boiler pressure at the designed working pressure all the time the engine is running, and both firing and water supply should be such that only when the engine not turning over at normal speed does the safety valve lift and release steam. Boilers that are constantly blowing off, i.e. when the pressure is 10% above the normal working pressure, are wasting valuable fuel. When the safety valve lifts, it is the time to put water into the boiler, so if hand pumping is used, watch for this moment. Also, of course, keep an eye on the water gauge to make sure that at all times there is sufficient water in the boiler to cover all flue tubes; a mark on or behind the gauge glass to indicate the minimum safe level will help this.

THROTTLES

Having now a more sophisticated power unit with control of the water intake, it behoves the builder to take care of control of the steam output, and again a simple screw-down type of valve will suffice. This should be connected in the steam line. The engine's supply can be cut off while steam is being raised to the designed working pressure and at any time during the period of operation. When radio control is considered then the screw-down valve can create problems in connecting it to the servo linkage and some use a taper plug cock as a control valve, with an extended handle on the plug. A more satisfactory idea is to use a disc-in-tube regulator as shown in figure 10.11.

LUBRICATION

When engines are continuously in operation, it is essential that the moving parts receive proper lubrication, especially the piston and cylinder. The most popular means of supplying oil to the cylinder is by a displacement lubricator, figure 10.12. This is a simple contrivance and depends for its operation on the fact that oil will float on water. When steam is admitted to the cylinder some will flow into the lubricator body, which being cold will cause the steam to con-

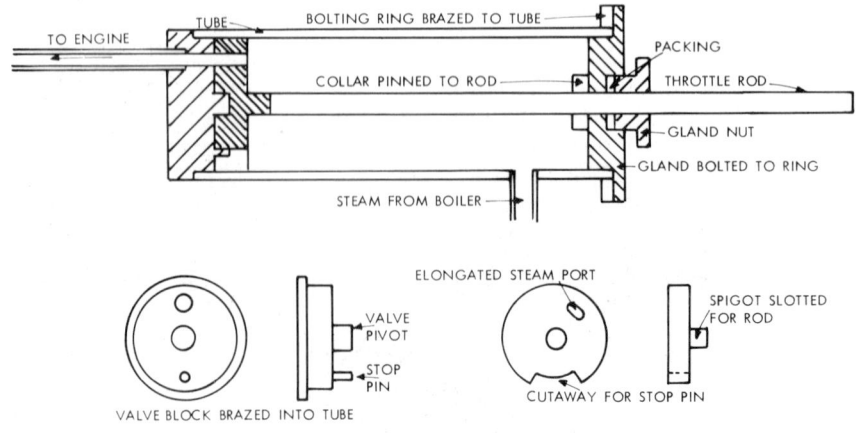

FIGURE 10.11

Auxiliaries

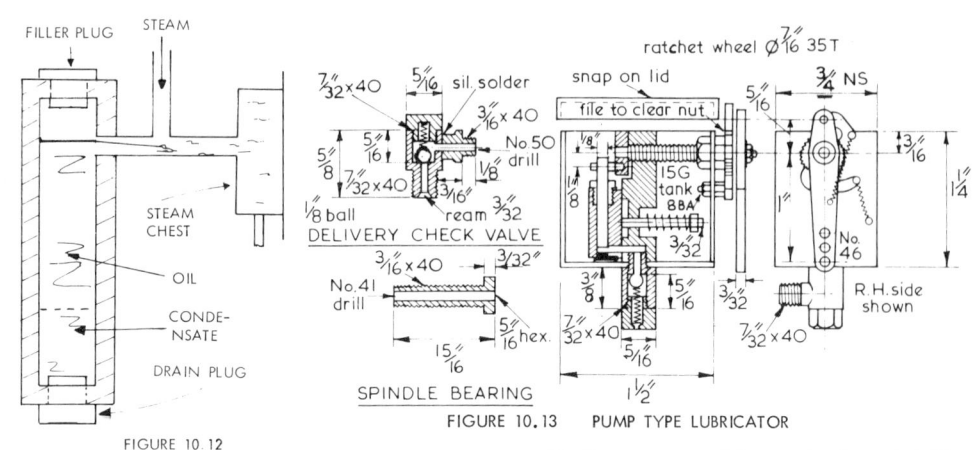

FIGURE 10.12

FIGURE 10.13 PUMP TYPE LUBRICATOR

dense. As the resulting condensate (water) sinks, oil will be displaced and flow into the steam moving into the cylinder.

A more efficient way of putting oil into the cylinder is to use a pump type lubricator as in figure 10.13. The oscillating pump, driven via its ratchet from the crosshead of the engine, can be arranged to provide a steady flow of oil all the time the engine is running. It has the advantage of being more easily refilled than a displacement lubricator, and also does not suffer from occasional gulps.

A Stuart Turner Sirius with flash steam boiler; pump is visible bottom left.

89

Introducing Model Marine Steam

FIGURE 10.14

FIGURE 10.15 SIMPLE OIL TRAP

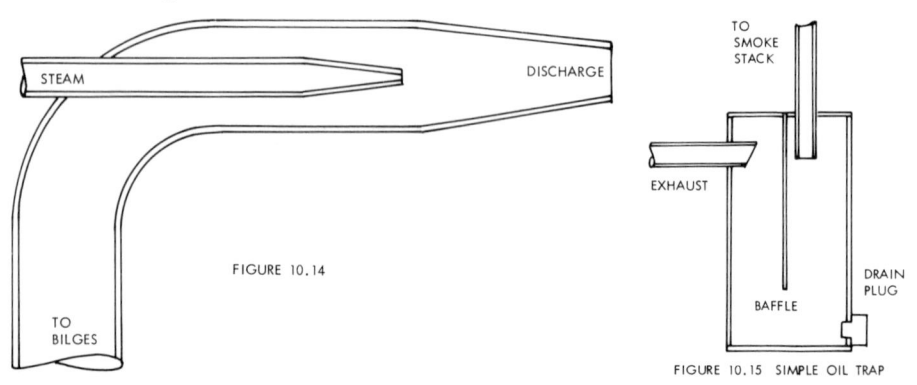

BILGE PUMPS AND EJECTORS

Any marine operation invariably means that some water will enter the hull and various means of clearing the water from the bilges are used, ranging from the brutal way of inverting the hull and letting the water run out by gravity, to more gentle ways, of which the most popular is to use a syringe and, on ending the run, to dry out with cloths. Not so often used are bilge pumps driven from the engine and these are the same type of pumps as used for boiler feed, except the intake is positioned at the lowest part of the hull and the discharge is via a pipe overboard. A version of the injector, much simplified as in figure 10.14, is sometimes used for the purpose, but both these mechanical aids are not very popular, as unless well constructed they can be more of a nuisance. In many cases the lakes on which boats operate are bound by local byelaws which prohibit ejecting oil-contaminated water into the lake.

OIL TRAPS

Consequent on the aforementioned byelaws, many model mariners fit oil traps to the exhausts of their boats. In the case where oil is kept at just the level required for efficient cylinder lubrication and no more, the oil contained in the exhaust can be burnt off by discharging up the funnel. Where added control of the used oil is needed or desired then the fitting of a simple exhaust oil trap as shown in figure 10.15 will take most of the oil out and make for a cleaner-running boat.

Chapter Eleven

Installation and Maintenance

Having decided on the boat and power plant, the builder is confronted with how to match one with the other, whether to copy prototypes and install each item of the power plant in separate compartments or to make the plant in one unit so that removal is easier. The type of boat being modelled has a great influence on the decision, for with many prototypes it will not be possible to arrange for a large part of the deck to be removed to give access to a unit type steam plant. On the other hand it will always be necessary to make some compromise with this problem, as is usual with the full size example, where many of the large items are broken down into smaller sections for installation. Engines are on occasion erected on shore, dismantled and re-erected on board. In modern day extreme cases the engine is built into the hull, and removal is only possible by cutting large parts of the hull away and re-welding after replacement. Neither of these two methods is practical in a model hull, so therefore one has to arrange that parts of the superstructure are made removable to gain access.

Generally the power plant of the launch type model is the one that will lend itself to the use of unit installations and in most other cases the builder will find that he has little option but to install each item separately. Having decided on the approximate position of each part of the installation, it is a good idea to check the balance of the hull before final fixing. This is done by floating the hull and then placing each part into its designed position. It may be found necessary to move the parts a little to obtain a water level parallel to the designed water line of the hull. Note that at this stage the hull should be floating high, even with all the parts in working order, i.e. with the boiler and fuel tank full. When the superstructure is complete, then is the time finally to ballast the model down to the required water line. Mark the positions determined by this test and check that the openings of the superstructure coincide with planned requirements of hull access, figure 11.1.

Having marked the position of the various items of the power plant, the next thing to do is to arrange fixings to the hull, remembering always that at some time or other the pieces will have to be removed for servicing; the boiler for retesting and the engine and pumps for re-packing of the glands, among other things. So arrange that all parts are screwed or bolted to brackets or beams in such a way that they can be removed with the aid of a single screwdriver or spanner. In the case of most items no

Introducing Model Marine Steam

FIGURE 11.1

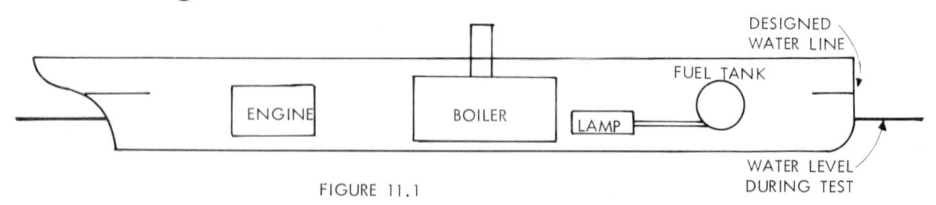

great ingenuity is required in the fixing arrangements; however, the one item that can be difficult is the engine itself, for this will have to be fitted so that the crankshaft lines up with the tail shaft of the boat or the primary shaft of a gearbox when fitted. For those who have recently graduated from the ranks of the fast i.c. engined boat, they will be pleased to learn that the engine can be fixed rigidly in the hull, for such is the beauty of steam, with an absence of objectionable noise, that such things as flexible noise insulating rubber mounts are not required. Most important, though, is the necessity to arrange the connection between engine and shaft so that minimum friction is created, and any inaccuracies in lining up initially or which develop because of hull movement should be taken care of in the drive arrangements at this stage.

Occasionally the crankshaft of the engine is made integral with the tail shaft, a design feature that cannot be recommended for general usage, if for no other reason than the fact that all hulls are liable to minor alterations to their shape in use at some time or other. This is particularly so in the case of wood hulls as the material ages, and in all cases because of the liability to damage while running or in transit. With this apparently simple arrangement any movement causing mis-alignment will add undue pressure, causing friction and wear to the shafting. A coupling that allows some flexibility between the two shafts is therefore required, and a type

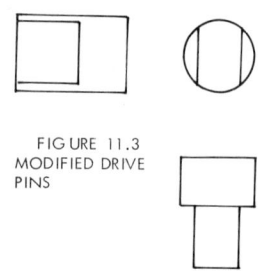

FIGURE 11.3
MODIFIED DRIVE PINS

that is in common use, having proved satisfactory over many years, is outlined in figure 11.2. Being easy to make is one of its virtues, but like all simple arrangements care in the making will pay a dividend. See that both drive discs are fitted firmly by screwing or brazing to their shafts; screw fixings can be made more secure by the use of Loctite or a similar modern adhesive. The drive

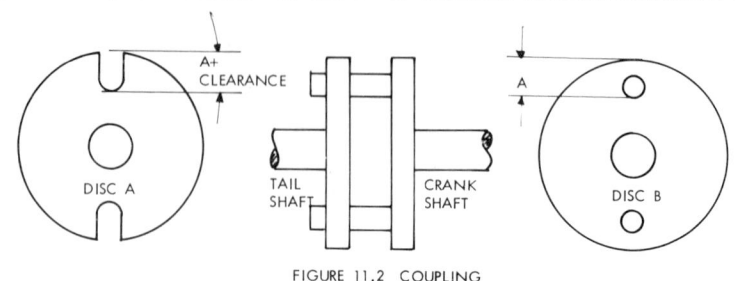

FIGURE 11.2 COUPLING

Installation and Maintenance

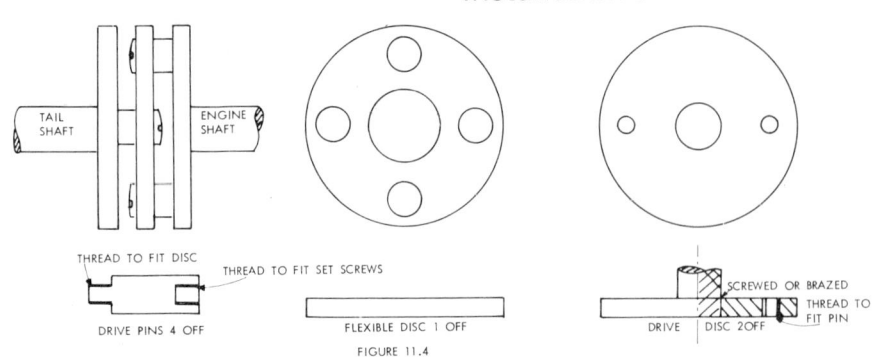

FIGURE 11.4 (labels: TAIL SHAFT, ENGINE SHAFT, THREAD TO FIT DISC, THREAD TO FIT SET SCREWS, DRIVE PINS 4 OFF, FLEXIBLE DISC 1 OFF, SCREWED OR BRAZED, THREAD TO FIT PIN, DRIVE, DISC 2 OFF)

pins need the same treatment and if a screw fixing is the method used, then some advantage in added life can be gained by case-hardening the pins and the driven disc. Elimination of some wear and a quieter drive can be obtained by making the drive pins larger and forming flats to fit the slot in the driven disc as in figure 11.3. In both cases a good working fit is needed between the pins and the slots so that there is the minimum of 'slap' and no suggestion of binding.

The many varieties of universal coupling sold in model shops for i.c. engined craft can also be used for connecting the two shafts together, and for those without workshop facilities is an easy method, while for the lucky ones there is no great effort in making their own. Figure 11.4 shows the layout of such a coupling, not to scale, but illustrating the general idea. While the use of such a coupling of the Hooke's joint type would seem to answer all problems in the lining up of the shafts, this is not so, for even with this coupling the centre line of the shafts must coincide at the centre point of the joint, figure 11.5, and if all misalignment is to be taken care of then two such joints are required on the drive line, figure 11.6.

So far it has been assumed that each unit of the steam plant is to be installed on its individual mounting in the hull, but in many cases it is possible and in-

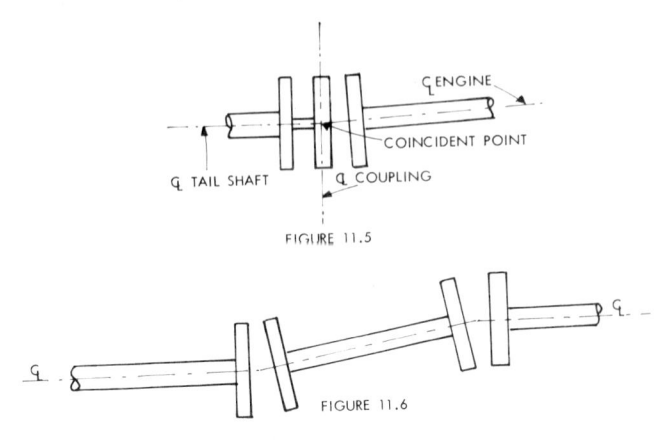

FIGURE 11.5 (labels: ₵ ENGINE, COINCIDENT POINT, ₵ TAIL SHAFT, ₵ COUPLING)

FIGURE 11.6

93

Introducing Model Marine Steam

Model engineering at its best; a flash steam engine in pristine condition seen at a recent Model Engineer Exhibition, by W. A. Bowie.

deed preferable to mount the whole plant on a sub-frame that can readily be removed from the hull. This sub-frame is a simple construction, usually of brass or aluminium alloy angle. Two side members, 'A' as in figure 11.7, are joined together with cross pieces 'B' by screwing, soft or, better, silver soldering, making a base on which to mount the various units. Often the cross pieces are dis-

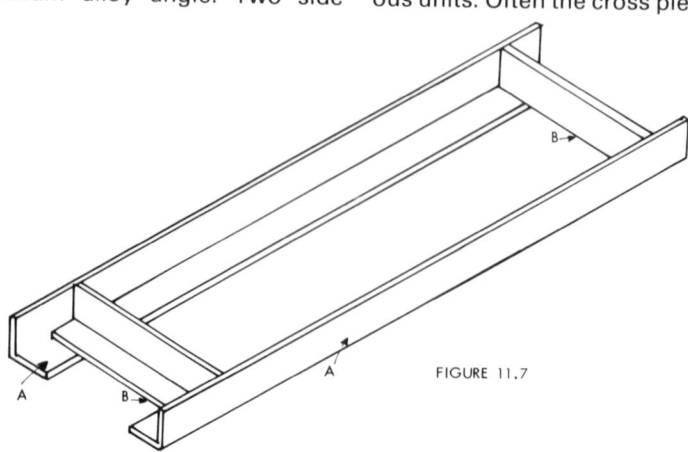

FIGURE 11.7

Installation and Maintenance

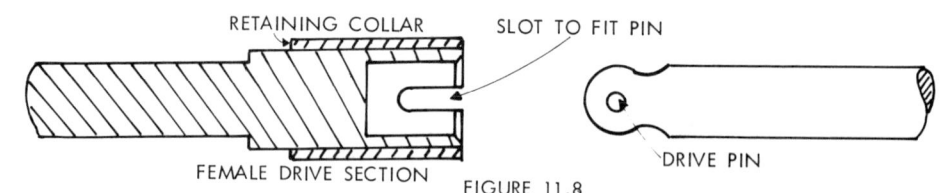

FIGURE 11.8 (RETAINING COLLAR, SLOT TO FIT PIN, FEMALE DRIVE SECTION, DRIVE PIN)

pensed with and the bases of the items used instead. The engine base is capable of taking the place of one cross member. The sub-frame is held to the hull with four or more fixing screws; usually the holes in the frame are at the corners and bushed, or fixing plates are mounted in the relevant places in the hull. The engine has to be lined up with the frame in position before the final fixing occurs, as it is essential that when the unit is taken out from the hull it will go back into exactly the same place each time.

To take care of any angularity between the shafts and to a lesser degree to allow some adjustment in case the two do not match each time the plant is replaced, a joint is required between the shafts and a common one in use is shown in figure 11.8. This consists of two parts, one of which has a ball end formed on it with a drive pin inserted crossways. The other part has a hole bored to the same diameter as the ball and a slot is made to match the pin. It is advisable to case-harden the pin, which can be made a force fit in the ball so that it can be renewed at any time, in which case the collar should be used to prevent the pin flying out in use. It is also advantageous to case-harden the drive collar of the female unit. It may seem contradictory to suggest the use of a single axis coupling in this case, but the amount of angularity and misalignment that is required to be overcome should be minimal, and the main requirement of the coupling other than the above is to make it easy to withdraw the power unit as a whole.

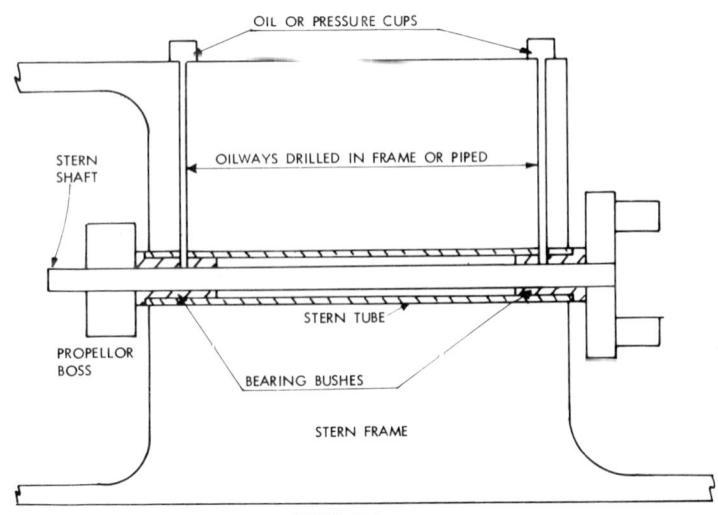

FIGURE 11.9 (OIL OR PRESSURE CUPS, STERN SHAFT, OILWAYS DRILLED IN FRAME OR PIPED, PROPELLER BOSS, STERN TUBE, BEARING BUSHES, STERN FRAME)

Introducing Model Marine Steam

In the majority of model steamers the thrust of the propeller is taken up by the rear bush of the stern tube, the stern shaft itself being run in two bushes in this tube without any means of lubrication being incorporated. While the elaborate stern tube arrangements of the prototype are not to be considered in our replicas, the lubrication needs should be taken care of by arranging that the bushes can be oiled or greased easily. An oiling arrangement as outlined in figure 11.9 is not difficult to install and if some form of thrust bearing can be included to take the force of the propeller, so much the better. In all cases, thrust from the propeller should never be taken up by the engine crankshaft, for this is a sure way to increase wear on the vital component. Bearing bushes in the arrangement outlined should be made of a reliable material such as cast bronze; it is worth noting that drawn metals should be eschewed for bearings if possible. Modern materials, e.g. PTFE, can be used with advantage in order to eliminate some of the lubrication problems, but avoid any that are affected by heat, as occasionally the steam plant will run in dry dock and sometimes the heat is transmitted to the rear shaft. If an oilite bearing can be found for this use so much the better, but remember that these bearings are formed by compression of sintered bronze powder and should not be machined. In short, design the stern arrangements around the available bushes and not the other way round.

Packing of the stern tube with thin grease and using some form of pressure cap, as used on bicycle hubs, will help towards keeping the stern tube assembly watertight, but so long as the various parts are good fits in the first place, and they are well maintained, leakage should be at a minimum. Incorporation of some form of gland is sometimes resorted to for larger models and in the smaller ones a bushing arrangement using felt washers as a seal can be useful.

MAINTENANCE

The completion of building a model steamer does not mean the end of all work on the project, for although a steam engine will continue to operate when it is in a deplorable state, it should be the owner's pride to keep the outfit in as good condition as is possible. Like all things mechanical, methodical maintenance is needed, both to ensure satisfactory running and also to rectify the result to wear and tear. Good maintenance will reduce the need for too early replacement of parts. It is not possible to over-emphasise the need for maintenance, and like the large steam plants of old, one that is installed in a model steamer and is kept clean and shiny indicates that the engineer/owner is taking good care of the equipment.

If the boiler is fitted with a blow-down valve, in effect a screw-down valve mounted at the lowest point of the boiler with an opening overboard, it is good policy to blow the boiler down at the end of each day's operation. By so doing, deposits in the boiler are cleared. It is not necessary to empty the boiler, although many make a practice of doing this, usually because some fitting is liable to leak. While the engine is still warm is the time to clean all oil, water and accumulated mess from the engine.

Also, empty the lubricator and generally clear all unwanted matter from the hull, taking care to get as much liquid from the bilges as is possible. If you do this with some heat in the boiler then oil and

Opposite, a clean and tidy installation featuring a Stuart Turner Double Ten engine and a return tube boiler.

Installation and Maintenance

Introducing Model Marine Steam

such like will be easier to remove than when cold, and in addition, after you have dried the hull as much as you can the residual heat will help the evaporation of anything left.

When cool, oil all the moving parts with light oil such as 3 in 1, to guard against rust. Also, put some steam oil into the cylinder. This last is most important if the cylinder is of iron, and it will be aided if the cylinders are fitted with a drain valve on the end as can be seen in some of the photographs. It is some people's practice to lift the safety valve and put a drop of oil on the stem to prevent corrosion. The practice arose because so-called stainless steel balls that appeared rustless were not so, and the safety valve seized up.

In the longer term there are certain operations that should be carried out on a regular basis, and perhaps the most important is that of boiler testing. All boilers should be tested to twice their working pressure before use and under current rules of most model associations the boiler should be retested to one and a half times that pressure each second year, as previously stated. While compliance with this rule is necessary to allow the owner to run a boat in competitions, it is not difficult to test the boiler each year for personal satisfaction. Retest of the boiler can be carried out with all the fittings except the safety valve in place, but at least once a year all the fittings should be removed and overhauled. With the fittings out, a few minutes work plugging the bushes and applying a hydraulic test will add to personal satisfaction as to the state of the boiler.

At this yearly check particular attention should be given to the state of the safety valve, renewing the springs and checking that it lifts at the correct pressure. Renew the glass of the water gauge if it is at all dirty, indeed for the small cost one can recommend a change irrespective of condition; renew the water gauge packing and check the condition of all the balls in non-return valves and replace at the first sign of wear. While the boiler is devoid of fittings, flush it through thoroughly with water to remove any loose deposit; it is known for some people to use a commercial water cleaner, or wash with killed spirits of salt at this time, and if this is done, make sure that afterwards the boiler is thoroughly cleaned with water to remove all trace of the cleansing agent.

At this annual check the engine should be taken apart and all parts checked for wear. Renew all the packing and reassemble, well oiling all moving parts ready for a steam-up at the beginning of the running season. If the boat is going to be out of use for a long period it sometimes pays to remove the engine, and after cleaning and oiling, pack it in a suitable box and keep in as dry a condition as practical. Many ships have been damaged through long storage in what is often the only place in the house, the garage, often suffering from condensation.

During the annual overhaul, check the blow-lamp if one is fitted, and if of the petrol/paraffin variety it is as well to remove the nipple and blow air through the piping, then replacing with a new nipple as soon as it is seen that the pipes are clear. If using a pressurised container treat it like the boiler and give it a check to one and half times working pressure. If as is advised the container is fitted with a pressure gauge, this and the one from the boiler should be checked against a master gauge.

During the running season pay attention to those items that aid safety – the water gauge, pressure gauges and the safety valves. If any one of these begins to give trouble take steps to rectify and if

Installation and Maintenance

Well known at Southern regattas are Olive Cockman and her steam yacht Victoria.

necessary replace rather than suffer inconvenience and a possible accident. At all times work to a pattern; this applies from the start of the run to the finish and for those who use blow-lamps remember that in the intital stages of warming up, they are more prone to flooding and emitting a stream of burning liquid than when under way. This flame thrower effect, while it may cause some amusement to the onlooker, is dangerous, for if someone is standing in tho way they can suffer burns. It is as well to point the lamp out over the water rather than inshore.

While it is common practice among many model engineers to bring their craft home and put them straight into their storage place, this is a procedure that is to be deplored, for a few minutes spent examining the craft in the workshop after an outing can often show some small item that requires attention. It is the cumulative effect of many small items that in the ultimate give rise to a major failure at the most important moment, which is always in front of the admiring crowd at the waterside.

99

Chapter Twelve

Experimentation and Radio Control

So the last chapter has been reached in this small book designed as a primer with the intent to arouse interest in the application of steam to the model ship. The steam engine has enjoyed such a vast field of use over the years that there is much that has been left out, but it is hoped that sufficient has been said to cause many of those who have read so far to go forth and follow the thoughts of the authors.

It will soon be obvious to those who make use of steam in model marine work that the medium has a lot of potential not touched upon, and no one should be afraid of trying something that to them or their colleagues is new or untried; experimenting even with the simplest of power plants can be both interesting and rewarding, but perhaps for the last time in these pages it must be said that whatever actions, variations of design or experiments our marine engineer does, the motto 'Safety first and always' should be the prime consideration.

Once having succumbed to the lure of the steam engine, our engineer will quickly make full use of the additional facilities that can add to his enjoyment and the pleasure and amusement of those who watch his activities. To the simple power unit all manner of additional facilities can soon be introduced, and with the addition of radio control, scope is practically unlimited. Possibly the first attraction is the provision of a steam whistle, and while this may appeal to the enthusiast, too much whistle on the wrong occasion can prove disturbing to others. Whistles are easily made, and figure 12.1 shows a general section of one commonly used.

With radio control the voyaging of our ships will become more realistic and it has to be remembered that the longer the cruise before a return to the lakeside, the more reliable the power unit has to be, and this is a case where good maintenance allied with a well thought out plant will provide the maximum enjoyment.

Following on the thoughts of extended cruising, many will attempt to improve the performance of their steam plants. Not just in the case of the seeker of high speed but with a more sedate plant, improvement always provides satisfaction and while the economics and consideration for conservation of fuel will not weigh heavily in most minds, many will try to obtain higher efficiency just because it offers a challenge, and who is to deny them their efforts? In the field of the small passenger-hauling locomotive the study of efficiency has paid dividends, better boilers and valve gear arrangements have given them more efficient results, and of course many of their precepts have

Experimentation, Radio Control

found favour in the model marine designs of today. So if experimentation is your bent go forth and may success come your way; you may be able to introduce improvements that will be of general benefit.

Experimentation to gain greater efficiency in a steam engine has often found an outlet in the development of the steam hydroplane, operated tethered by a line to a central pivot, and for those who follow this line, be warned, it is a hard road with few success being recorded. Indeed it has been likened to 'hitting one's head against a brick wall', with few bricks dislodged and the wall still standing. Problems that have to be overcome are many; the need for a high performance engine with adequate lubrication functioning under extreme high pressures, maybe 200lbs/sq.in.; the difficulty of providing a water supply to a machine gyrating at perhaps 60 plus m.p.h. and continually breaking contact with the water; a similar problem in getting the heat source to function continually under the same conditions. The determined, and those with a yen for a challenge, will not be discouraged by these words; the way is wide open for fresh thinking and who knows, even if complete success is not achieved some fundamental idea can emerge to benefit many others.

But to return to the more common use of steam in the slower and quieter running craft, many of the auxiliaries that are operated by electricity in boats propelled by that medium could be run from the steam supply; such items as winches, fire pumps and the like would all operate by steam, only requiring simple multi-cylinder (oscillating?) engines to provide the motive power. Control by radio would be simple and only require the coupling of a control valve to a servo on a spare channel.

Perhaps a few words on the type of radio control equipment available and some hints and tips about its installation would be useful at this point.

HOW MANY FUNCTIONS?

Many newcomers to radio control become confused with channels and functions. The term channel is a hangover from the reed and tone system days, an earlier form of radio control, where one channel oscillated one reed or tone, which moved the servo mechanism in one direction only. Therefore, for a typical boat installation of rudder and speed control, you needed four channels, i.e. left and right rudder and slow and fast throttle. The maximum number of channels was 12.

Most of today's gear is proportional equipment and here we use the term

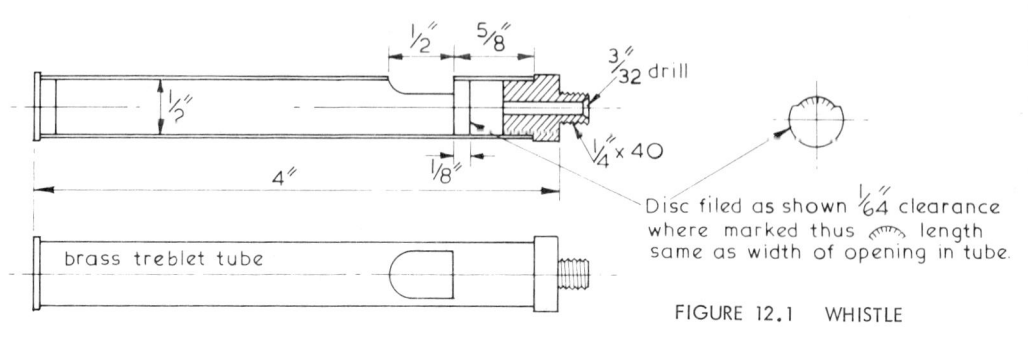

FIGURE 12.1 WHISTLE

Introducing Model Marine Steam

Fig. 12·2 A typical modern two-function radio. The large unit is the transmitter, and the receiver, two servos, switch and battery pack are carried in the model.

'function' to describe the total movement of one control surface, i.e. one function will control the entire rudder movement and a second function will control the entire speed range required, figure 12.2.

It is obvious therefore, that many boat requirements can be met by a two function outfit, but we would recommend purchase of a four or even six function outfit for the dedicated steam enthusiast as the time will soon come when extra functions will be called upon to handle lights, winches, anchors, horns, whistles, fire monitors etc.; the list is endless. Of course there is a snag. Money. More functions mean more expense. However, it is possible to buy an expandable two function or a four function outfit with only two of the servos, adding the others at a later date as and when necessary. It is very important to consider these possible future intentions, as some sets of two function gear are non-expandable – i.e., they cannot be extended to operate extra servos.

Radio is so compact now that it can be fitted into most model boats, including many plastic kits. Nevertheless, beginners are advised to build something reasonable large for a start, and a suggested rule of thumb is that if you

102

Experimentation, Radio Control

multiply the beam in inches times the length and obtain a figure greater than 120, you should have little difficulty. However, most steam boats will be large enough to accept the steam plant, and finding ample space for the radio gear should not prove a problem.

In most models of this size factor and over, it should be possible to install all the radio gear, i.e. receiver, batteries and servos at least, in a waterproof compartment and ideally in a waterproof container. Dampness is the arch-enemy of radio equipment, and protection from this and steam vapour is especially important with steam powered models. An obvious statement perhaps, but the number of model boaters who allow their radio gear literally to float in water is beyond belief. Suggest that they operate their portable television or cassette player in the rain and you get a very odd look, but to our minds there is no difference in principle.

A very popular choice for a container to take all boat radio gear is one of the large variety of lunchbox/food containers obtainable from multiple stores. These usually have a flush fitting lid and can easily be sealed with good quality adhesive tape. Alternatively, you can purchase purpose-made boxes from your model shop available in a variety of shapes and sizes and usually supplied with switch, charging sockets, aerial socket, mounting brackets etc.

The only disadvantage with mounting the whole 'works' in one container is that whereas the receiver and batteries can be surrounded by foam for anti-vibration and protection against impact, the servos need to be firmly fitted to the box to avoid sloppy control systems. The box must be firmly fixed to the model of course. Also, make sure that effective linkages can be arranged to the rudder, throttle, switches etc.

In the model at right, all the radio is stowed in the bow away from heat and steam. Rudder is operated by a 'snake' which runs above deck.

Introducing Model Marine Steam

The radio in this tug model is under a screwed lid seen aft. Inset, the home-built steering motor is next to the radio box (figure shows position). Note the blower on the boiler uptake, indicating that the model is fired by solid fuel.

The problem with small equipment is that one is encouraged to build even smaller models and in many cases it is impossible to group the equipment together because of space limitations, and the servos have to be mounted separately. In this case try to provide a watertight compartment and mount them as high as possible, away from the bilge water, and clear of splashes or seepage that finds its way up rudder posts.

The disadvantage with separately mounted servos is the extra time and

Experimentation, Radio Control

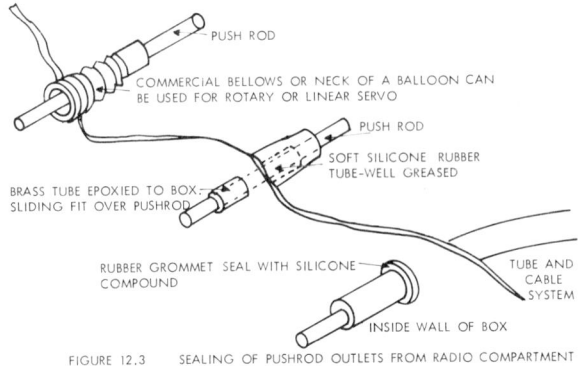

FIGURE 12.3   SEALING OF PUSHROD OUTLETS FROM RADIO COMPARTMENT

fiddling required when changing the equipment to another model, unless of course you can afford separate servos for each model and simply change over the receiver and battery box.

WATERPROOFING TECHNIQUES

The easiest system to deal with is the plastic lunchbox or commercial variant which, as has already been stated, can be sealed with adhesive tape or with a screw-down top onto a soft sponge or rubber-covered flange. The small openings necessary to allow exiting of pushrods, switch operating rod and aerial can be sealed with rubber grommets, balloon necks, silicone, rubber compound etc., as shown in figure 12.3. Without doubt, linear servos are best for

Fig. 12·4 A food-box type radio box installed in a sealed-off compartment covered by a bolt-on see-through hatch. Servos are separately mounted.

105

Introducing Model Marine Steam

such installation as one does not have to take into account the rotary displacement of a push-rod.

If size or layout prohibits the use of the ubiquitous plastic box, receiver and batteries can be enclosed in polythene bags with all wires exiting through the neck of the bag, which is then tightly bound with elastic bands and/or adhesive tape. The only problem is that a completely sealed package will give rise to condensation inside the bag. However, this can be eliminated by placing a sachet of silica gel, a crystallised absorbent, in the bag. This chemical has excellent powers of water absorption, but obviously after some weeks becomes saturated and needs removing and drying out in a warm oven or on top of a radiator.

As previously mentioned, separately mounted servos should be well above the bilges and away from obvious points of water ingress such as hatch coamings and rudder posts. If you have the availability of waterproof servos which are sealed at the manufacturers, then all well and good, but beware of those advertised as water-resistant. There is a world of difference between resistant to water and proofed against water. One method of achieving reasonable water-resistance is to open the servo case carefully and smear a thin film of impact adhesive or silicone gasket solution on the case joints and at the point where the wires emerge. These substances can easily be peeled away when maintenance becomes necessary. A further point to watch is, if the fixing screws enter the bottom of the case, these should be treated with blobs of silicone grease. The latter substance can also be used around the output arm.

There are many ways of producing water-resistant and even water-proofed compartments within a model to accept the separate installation method, ranging from sliding hatches to quick-fasten screws. For large models with a high freeboard these are more than adequate, but for small models that may

Visible aft of the engine in this model are battery box, receiver, and servos, one clearly for rudder and the other operating a throttle via a long push-rod.

106

Experimentation, Radio Control

be frequently awash one of the more positive methods is the bolt-down hatch arrangement, figure 12.4. The radio compartment is first sealed off from the rest of the boat by bulkheads glued or resined into position. The resulting box is then rimmed with 1/2in. square wooden strips, finishing slightly proud of the deck. This coaming is draw-filed with a large flat file to achieve a level surface. The hatch cover is fabricated from 1/8in. Perspex or acrylic sheet, which can be purchased in a variety of colours from hardware merchants. Drill clearance holes around the edge of the sheet, at approximately 2 1/2in to 3in. centres, to accommodate 5/8in. by No.8 self tapping screws. Use the cover as a template to drill 3/32in. holes in the wood coaming and carefully drive the screw home. When fitting the cover during normal use, smear a thin film of silicone grease over the coaming and as the hatch is screwed down and the surfaces come together, a clear indication of a good seal is apparent. An alternative to grease is to shape and fit a thin rubber sealing gasket. The object of the transparent sheet of course, is to enable a rapid visual inspection to be carried out for watertightness.

Fast access to the radio compartment is restricted with any system which includes some degree of screw fixing, as it does take two or three minutes to gain entry, but surely this disadvantage is more than justified by the guarantee of absolute dryness. A further refinement with this system is to fit a Schräder car tyre valve in the hatch and apply a few pounds of air from a hand pump before sailing. The positive pressure within the compartment will effectively prevent any water ingress.

This simple Mamod-powered model uses a waterproof rudder servo and wraps the rest of the radio in a plastic bag with a silica gel sachet. Model by John Cheesman, photo by John Torrance.

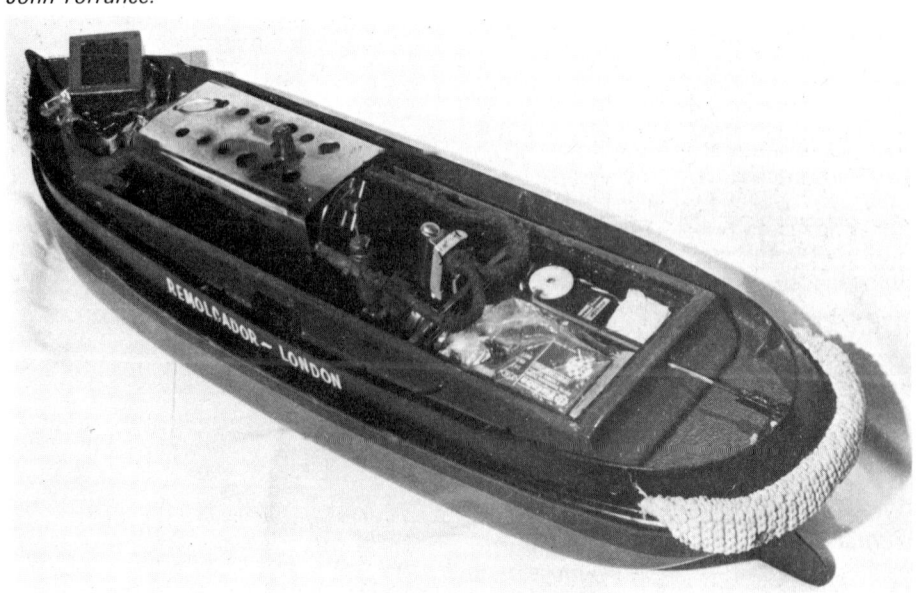

Introducing Model Marine Steam

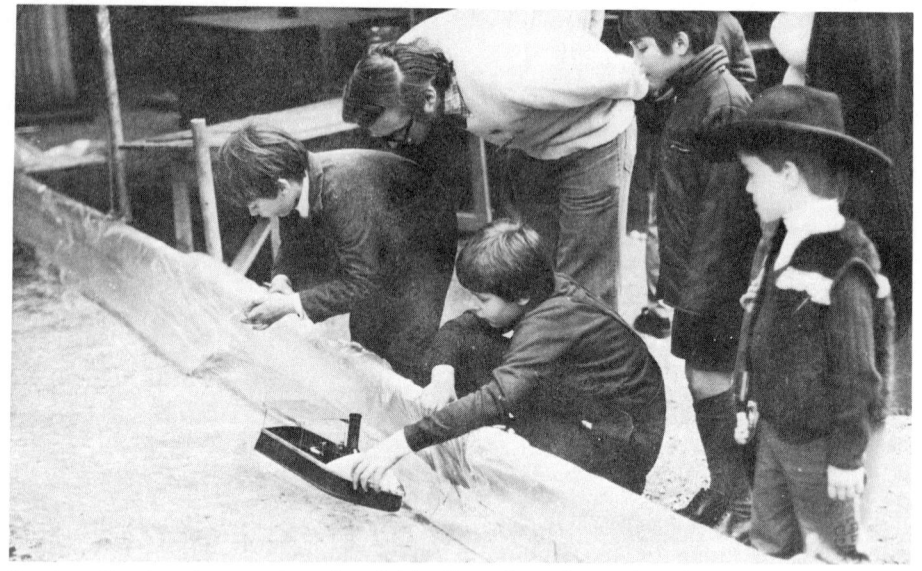

Young enthusiasts intrigued at a Kew Bridge Trust Open Steam Day. Once bitten, the bug can last a lifetime. Opposite, enthusiasts at a St. Albans International.

DRYING OUT

If the worst does happen and everything gets soaked, the first thing to do is disconnect the batteries. It is the electrolytic effect and short circuits which cause the most damage. Most of the solid state components used in radio gear will not be affected by a short dunking in fresh water, but salt water is a different situation entirely. The best action to take in the latter case is to dunk receivers and servos in a bucket of fresh water or rinse them under a cold tap. Drastic action, but you must remove all traces of salt otherwise within a few days you will have a green rotting mass. After flushing, blow out as much water as possible and then borrow a hair dryer for final drying out. There will still be a problem in that the small motors used in the servos are made to such tight tolerances that moisture will remain trapped inside. They cannot be taken apart without special equipment. However, don't despair, modern technology will help. No self-respecting modeller should be without a can of instant maintenance; examples are WD40 and AP75, obtainable at most motor accessory shops. These liquids penetrate, repel moisture, clean and lubricate, and a quick squirt will cure the motor problem. The stuff will also work miracles with dirty plugs, switches, telescopic aerials, linkages etc.

SWITCH ACCESS

The switch between battery and the receiver is often the weak point in a waterproofing system utilising the plastic container, but is an essential item when quick access to the receiver/battery plug and socket is denied. Two methods have found favour over the years. The switch can be operated by a wire push rod

Experimentation, Radio Control

which passes through a close-fitting grease filled bush mounted in the side of the radio box. Alternatively, large rubber blind plugs can be obtained from motor accessory shops and fitted immediately above the switch in either the radio box lid or the deck/hatch of a waterproof compartment. They are extremely easy and quick to remove and replace and are completely watertight when their rubber lips are smeared with a thin film of silicone grease.

Combined with radio control, or indeed without it perhaps, can come the interesting designing of fully automatic water supplies to the boiler by regulating the operation of the feed pump by means of either a mechanical water level check or more probably by using an electronic sensor to open and close the bypass valve. Already some have placed a sensor in the water gauge to generate a signal to a transistorised control circuit which operates either a control valve or a separate electric pump, but the true steam man will have no dealings with this foreign power except as a means of relaying the findings of his system of check. Automatic regulation of the fuel supply is another aspect of operation that can well be usefully explored and if liquefied gas is used as fuel then the problem will be resolved much more easily than if other fuels are used.

The steam engine may be old hat to many, but there is an undeniable fascination about steam that endures. Perhaps it is because that off all motive power types, steam is the one that appears to have some human quality and it is fitting to close this book as we opened it with just those thoughts, and the knowledge that once bitten, few people can avoid a continual interest in the steam engine. So, go forth and enjoy one of the most popular addictions of mankind – the steam engine!

Appendix 1.

PROPERTIES OF STEAM AND RELATIONSHIPS BETWEEN FUELS AND POWER.

The basic unit is the British Thermal Unit (B.T.U.):- the amount of heat necessary to raise the temperature of 1lb of water through 1°F. In ideal conditions, one B.T.U. would produce 778ft.lb. of energy; i.e., enough energy to raise a weight of 1lb. a height of 778ft. or vice-versa.

As an example, to raise 1lb. of water from say 58°F to its boiling point at normal atmospheric pressure which is 212°F, requires (212° − 58°) = 154 B.T.U.s. To convert this pound of water to steam will require a further 971 B.T.U.s and this latter quantity is known as the latent heat of vaporisation. Further heat will raise the pressure above atmospheric.

Suppose we could have an ideal engine, capable of changing all the heat from its burning fuel into mechanical energy. If this engine burned coal whose heat of combustion is 12,000 B.T.U./lb., a typical figure, how many pounds would it have to burn each minute to develop 1hp.? 1lb of coal yields 12,000 x 778 = 9,336,000. ft.lbs. The long established figure for 1 hp is 33,000 ft,lbs. of work per minute, hence pounds of coal required = $\frac{33{,}000}{9{,}336{,}000}$ = 0.00354 lbs per minute.

This is equivalent to about 0.2 lbs/hr. for 1h.p. per hour, or 1lb. of coal should produce around 4.7 hp. for one hour. In actual fact a good reciprocating engine and steam plant will produce around 1 hp per hour for a consumption of about 1½ lb. of coal which, in an ideal engine/plant, should produce over 8 hp. Hence the thermal efficiency is approx. 12% The efficiency of a full size steam locomotive is of the order of 8 to 12%. Stationary power plants using reciprocating engines have efficiencies of 15 − 20%, while plants using turbines and condensers have efficiencies that reach around 35%. The development of more efficient types of engines and plants would do much to conserve our reserve supply of fuels, hence experimentation and development work by marine model engineers is not out of place in today's world.

Calculation of Theoretical H.P. of an Engine. The formula for calculating the theoretical h.p. for a reciprocating engine is;

$$HP = \frac{P \times L \times A \times N}{33{,}000}$$

where P = mean effective pressure in the cylinder in lbs.sq.in.
    L = stroke of piston in feet
    A = area of piston in sq.in
    N = number of strokes per min. in a double acting engine.

Note that due to losses in pipes, inlet passages, etc., P is usually approx ½ the boiler pressure and also that the formula does not take into account frictional losses which are relatively large in a small engine. Usually, the power given out at the crankshaft approaches ⅔ of the calculated theoretical horse-power.

Appendix 2.

USEFUL FACTS AND FIGURES.

Length
- 1 inch = 2.54 centimetres
- 1 foot = 30.479 centimetres
- 1 yard = 0.9144 metre
- 1 centimetre = 0.393 inch
- 1 metre = 3.28 feet

Area
- 1 sq.in. = 6.45 sq. centimetres
- 1 sq.ft. = 9.29 sq. decimetres
- 1 sq.yd. = 0.836 sq. metre
- 1 sq. metre = 10.763 sq.ft.

Volume
- 1 cu.in = 16.387 cu. centimetres
- 1 cu. foot = 0.028 cu. metre
- 1 gallon = 4.545 litres
- 1 litre = 1.76 pints
- 1 cu.cm = 0.061 cu. inch
- 1 cu. metre = 35.314 cu. feet

Weight
- 1 pound = 0.453 kilogramme
- 1 kilogramme = 2.205 lb.

Imperial to Metric:
- Inches × 2.54 = centimetres
- Yards × 0.9144 = metres
- Gallons × 4.546 = litres
- Pounds × 0.4536 = kilogrammes

Miscellaneous: One gallon of water weighs 10lbs., contains 277 cu.ins., or 4.54 litres.
One litre of water contains 61 cu.ins, weighs 2.2 lbs. or 1 kilogramme.
One knot = 1 nautical mile per hour.
One nautical mile = 1.1528 statute miles.
One cu.ft of water weighs 62.42 lbs. and contains 6.24 gallons.
One pound of water contains 27.7 cu.in. or 1/10 of a gallon.

Weights of Materials: Approximate weight of one cu.inch:
- Aluminium 0.09 lb.
- Brass 0.30 lb.
- Cast Iron 0.26 lb.
- Copper 0.32 lb.
- Lead 0.41 lb.
- Nickel 0.31 lb.
- Steel 0.28 lb.